# Lesbian and Gay Issues

## A Resource Manual for Social Workers

Hilda Hidalgo

Travis L. Peterson

Natalie Jane Woodman

editors

National Association of Social Workers
Silver Spring, Maryland

*Designed by Joan Stoliar*

Copyright © 1985, National Association of Social Workers, Inc.

**Library of Congress Cataloging in Publication Data**

Main entry under title:

Lesbian and gay issues.

    Bibliography: p.
     1. Social work with homosexuals—United States—Addresses, essays, lectures.   2. Homosexuality—United States—Addresses, essays, lectures.  I. Hidalgo, Hilda. II. Peterson, Travis L.   III. Woodman, Natalie Jane, 1931–
HV1449.L47   1984           362.8            84-25585
ISBN 0-87101-127-1

Printed in U.S.A.

LOCAL 229

# Dedication

The editors and contributors dedicate this manual to the many lesbian founders of our profession and most especially to Jane Addams. This great woman-identified woman led social work in its obligations to counteract oppression and injustice with liberation and empowerment. For too long, the profession has acclaimed her leadership as a social change agent while denying that her lesbian identification existed as a major influence in her life, her work, and her understanding of oppression.

This manual is a forward move toward liberation of lesbians and gays, changing the homophobic social work attitudes and behaviors of social service institutions and social work practice. It also provides the opportunity to open a "historical closet" and acknowledge Jane Addams in her whole personhood.

# Foreword

The profession of social work has a long and respected history of commitment to justice and human dignity. The National Association of Social Workers has been a primary vehicle through which the commitments of the profession are translated into clear policy and action.

Consistent with the profession's commitment and the Association's responsibility, NASW has sought to further human understanding and combat injustice as related to lesbians and gays in our nation and to address social work practice issues as applied to gays and lesbians.

This manual represents one means toward our increased understanding and improved practice on behalf of our lesbian and gay constituents and clients.

Robert P. Stewart, ACSW
*NASW President*

# Preface

This resource manual is a publication that few of us who have been involved in its production can view with complete objectivity. The women and men who comprised the first NASW National Task Force on Lesbian and Gay Issues recognized the need for such a manual. Because of their own experiences as social workers, they were very aware of the homophobia rampant in their profession. They well knew the biased, prejudiced view of homosexuality and homosexuals in their social work education. They were equally well aware of the treatment of homosexuals in the social welfare system, whether the homosexual was a client or colleague. Perhaps some were aware of their own homophobia and had ambivalence about being "the first out of the closet."

As I perceive it, the Editorial Advisory Committee responsible for the contents of this manual had two agendas: one overt and one hidden. First and foremost, the purpose of this manual is to help social work practitioners to become more effective in their practice with clients who "happen to be homosexual." An equally important purpose, but one still having to be hidden, is to offer homosexual social workers a way of gaining a better feeling about themselves.

There is no question that Jane Addams and many of our other social work "foremothers" depended on the support of their same-gender colleagues. They established close personal relationships that strengthened them to achieve their professional goals. Acknowledging this tradition has become a feminist and a lesbian and gay issue. Unfortunately, up to now, history has, for the most part, been recorded by white Anglo-Saxon men who are products of their culture.

My hope for the value of this manual is that social workers may become better practitioners: more sensitive to the needs of their clients, more skilled in their practice, and more assertive in their advocacy in both the microsystems and macrosystems in which they are involved. The civil rights movement recognized the importance of the statement "black is beautiful." This manual says "it's OK to be gay."

Josephine H. Stewart, Chair
*NASW National Committee on Lesbian and Gay Issues*

# Acknowledgments

Our gratitude to the Program Advancement Fund of NASW that provided the seed monies needed for the development of this resource manual. Our very special thanks to the many volunteer social workers and other professionals who joined the editors in freely donating their knowledge and expertise (the Editorial Advisory Committee, the contributing authors, the researchers, reviewers, typists, and proofreaders). We regret that space does not allow us to list each of them individually.

The editors hope that this manual will be a small—but important—tool for social workers to use in evaluating past omissions and inaccuracies about gay men and lesbians. This resource manual is an expression of the commitment and dedication that the editors and all the persons that contributed to this effort have toward a goal of a humanistic, pluralistic, nonoppressive society for humankind.

# Committees

### Editorial Advisory Committee

Hilda Hidalgo, PhD, MSW, ACSW *(co-editor)*
Travis L. Peterson, MSW, ACSW *(co-editor)*
Natalie Jane Woodman, MSS, ACSW *(co-editor)*
David Aronstein, MSW
John Grace, MSW
Jennifer Parkes, MSW

### NASW National Task Force on Lesbian and Gay Issues (1979–82)

Larry Davis, MSW, ACSW *(co-chair)*
Bernice Goodman, MS, ACSW *(co-chair)*
Kenneth Eisenberger, MSW, ACSW
Hilda Hidalgo, PhD, MSW, ACSW
Travis L. Peterson, MSW, ACSW

Thom Gauthier, AM, ACSW *(staff)*

### NASW National Committee on Lesbian and Gay Issues (1982–present)

Josephine H. Stewart, MSW, ACSW *(chair)*
Gloria Donadello, PhD, MSW, ACSW
Gary W. Drake, MSW, ACSW
Lawrence D. Farrell, MSW, ACSW
Manuel F. Fimbres, PhD, MSW, ACSW
Patricia L. Gunter, PhD, MSW
Barry L. Moore, MSW, ACSW
Liz Simon, MSW, ACSW
Natalie Jane Woodman, MSS, ACSW

Thom Gauthier, AM, ACSW *(staff)*

# Contents

## SECTION I
### Populations at Risk—Interventive Strategies

**SECTION II**
Macro Intervention

# SECTION III
## Professional Relationships and Professional Development

## APPENDIXES

**APPENDIXES** *(continued)*

## RESOURCES

## ABOUT THE EDITORS AND AUTHORS

# Introduction
## Hilda Hidalgo, Travis L. Peterson, and Natalie Jane Woodman

As recently as the 1950s and 1960s, hardly the Middle Ages, the *Diagnostic and Statistical Manual of Mental Disorders* of the American Psychiatric Association (APA), used extensively by mental health practitioners, listed homosexuality as a "sexual deviation" and classified homosexuals with people who committed antisocial or destructive crimes, child molesters, voyeurs, and exhibitionists.[1]

Then in the 1970s, only a few years later, the APA removed homosexuality from the list of mental disorders; the American Public Health Association deplored all public and private discrimination against lesbians and gay men and urged all health agencies to educate staff and workers on relevant issues; and, in 1977, our own National Association of Social Workers (NASW) affirmed "the right of all persons to define and express their own sexuality," and vowed to "combat archaic laws. . .and other forms of discrimination which serve to impose something less than equal status upon the homosexually-oriented members of the human family."[2] Obviously, homosexuals had come a long way in a relatively short time.

But why then did Señora María Ramos write, "Now it is too late for Ovidio. . ." about her son who killed himself as a result of Anita Bryant's hate campaign against homosexuals?[3] Why can a lover or friend of 20 years be excluded from an intensive care unit or be denied participation in decisions involving life-or-death medical situations, while a relative

---

[1] American Psychiatric Association, *Diagnostic and Statistical Manual of Mental Disorders* (1st ed.; Washington, D.C.: Mental Hospitals Service, 1952) (2d ed.; Washington, D.C.: APA, 1968).

[2] See Appendix B for text of NASW Public Social Policy Statement on Gay Issues.

[3] Bernice Goodman, *Confronting Homophobia* (National Gay Health Coalition Educational Foundation, 1978), p. 11.

who hasn't seen the patient in as many years is allowed to visit and make such vital decisions? Why are adults still jailed for engaging privately in homosexual practices, and gays and lesbians legally denied both public and private employment? And most important of all, at least to us as social workers, why must lesbians and gays and persons important in their lives still avoid or delay until too late obtaining needed help because our social work institutions are known for a lack of knowledge, an absence of relevant skills, and the existence of blatant hostility to alternative lifestyles?

Clearly, although homosexuals have "come a long way," they still have a long way to go. It is hoped that this manual, prepared for helping professionals as a group and social workers in particular, will (1) provide insight, information, resources, and bibliographical references; (2) increase social workers' skills in working with lesbians and gays; and (3) ameliorate attitudes that have impeded awareness, outreach, and effective intervention with this oppressed minority.

**Organization and Interrelationship of Sections in This Manual** The reader will note that the organizing theme of combatting oppression in order to facilitate growth and development intrapersonally and within larger systems has been addressed by the authors. Although many of the principles are basic to the helping process, it is the overriding factor of homophobia (fear, dislike, and hatred of homosexuals and homosexuality) that makes intervention sufficiently unique to warrant this manual.

At the outset, the reader is introduced to relevant terminology in the Glossary. Section I provides an overview of the populations under consideration, issues of concern to these clients, and suggestions for treatment.

But social workers must also be sensitive to the implications of societal oppression of clients and examine attitudes toward social change and advocacy. Our Code of Ethics enjoins us all—gays and nongays alike—to ameliorate persecution at all levels of society. Thus, following this attention to "microsystems"—that is, intervention with individuals or small groups who are parts of lesbian/gay subpopulations— the following sections (II, II, and the Appendixes) ask us to consider change roles in "macrosystems." The Resources including References by Content Area provide further information for the professional who wishes to pursue further learning relative to lesbians and gays.

Authors of articles in all the sections emphasize that working with lesbian and gay clients requires awareness of and sensitivity to the problems affecting this oppressed minority, and, as mentioned, special knowledge, skill, and attitudes.

## Knowledge

The social work practitioner should have some background awareness of historical perspectives as they affect gays and lesbians. This includes not only religious and legal oppression but also the travesties of "treatment" imposed by the helping professions (the readings suggested in References by Content Area may help to put to rest the myths that underlie a "pathology and cure" approach to helping).

Another important dimension of knowledge is that of insight into contemporary gay and lesbian communities and the resources available through informal and formal networks. This is necessary in helping the client to bridge the gap from "closet" to agency to peer interaction. Such awareness will also provide an understanding of the wide range of lesbian/gay lifestyles (individually and in coupled relationships) and minimize the tendency toward stereotyping.

Finally, the worker should be cognizant of the fact that gayness and lesbianism apply to a total orientation and be able to move away from the emphasis on homosexuality. Such an orientation has ramifications for individuals throughout the life span of development and is accompanied by greater or lesser degrees of stress. These stresses more usually than not are tied to oppression within a homophobic society; therefore, intervention requires more than a strictly intrapersonal focus.

## Skills

Most of the basic precepts of the helping process have very special applicability in working with the lesbian or gay client. For example, the dictum of "starting where the client is" requires that the worker not assume that all clients are "upset" about their orientations or that this is the underlying "cause" for any presenting problem. Many lesbians and gays feel joyful in their lifestyles, but may seek help because of such situational crises as loss of a lover, death of a parent or child, or economic stress. Throughout the first section, authors have focused on these various problems that individuals may undergo.

Another basic precept is the ethical responsibility of the social worker in supporting the client's right to self-determination. With lesbians and gays, this is clearly related to the right to be aware of the self and same-sex orientation and not be subjected to the worker's definition of "healthy" or "appropriate" behaviors. This applies not only to the frequent practice of approaching clients with a treatment plan to change the client's orientation (an unworkable goal) but also to changing the client's mannerisms. For example, to impose on the client the expectation that he/she will conform to a new supermacho or superfeminine image that is not a part of self-definition is unethical.

Finally, listening to the client and accepting the client's problem definition reinforces the client's capacity for self-acceptance. It eliminates the potential for the worker, and, consequently, the client or significant others, to fall into the trap of believing that to be gay or lesbian is sick, bad, crazy, or evidence of incompetence.

### Attitudes

Probably no other dimension of the helping process received more attention from the authors than concern for the need to give attention to one's own preconceptions, misconceptions, and biases. It cannot be overemphasized that social workers must examine their own attitudes prior to working with gay/lesbian clients. We all have been socialized in a homophobic society, but it is an ethical imperative that we reassess ourselves, even as this has been necessary in such areas as racism and sexism.

Lesbians and gays repeatedly state that it is not the sexual orientation of a therapist that matters so much as the professional's competence and attitudes. Many of us received our training in a "pathology oriented" model, and some of us have not reexamined the implications of this, particularly as it relates to working with lesbians and gays. Now is the time to do so.

### In-House Training

By combining the materials and suggestions provided in Section III, Appendixes, and Resources with other parts of the manual, the agency that wishes to provide training can develop programs that include:

- information and research about lesbian/gay history and lifestyles;
- training materials that support viewing homosexuality and lesbian/gay lifestyles as healthy;
- exercises helpful in values clarification and in the identification of homophobic feelings and attitudes; and
- exercises helpful in heightening consciousness and changing negative feelings, attitudes, and behaviors toward lesbians and gays.

The material presented is adaptable and can be used by individuals in a self-educating process as well as by groups in structured in-service training sessions and institutes. Suggestions about possible use of the material for group and individual activities are provided.

It is important that group leaders prepare and structure training events to ensure quality and an atmosphere that allows participants' expression of feelings and beliefs about lesbians and gays as a step in eradicating fears and negative attitudes. Whenever possible, openly gay and lesbian professionals should be used as trainers, presenters, and facilitators. Trainers (lesbian, gay, or nongay) must be in touch with their own homophobia and be aware of how it affects their performance as trainers.

Among the materials provided in the Appendixes is a sample of a brief outline, prepared by the Committee on Lesbian and Gay Issues of the Virginia NASW Chapter, that other chapters can use to request in-service training and events. A Trainer's (Facilitator's) Planning Work Sheet is also included to ensure that all aspects of a well-planned training session are addressed by the responsible parties. Workshop ideas and topics are also suggested in the Peterson selection on continuing education.

In the area of professional relationships, identifying and reassessing interactional patterns are essential. Grace's chapter discusses the importance of lesbian and gay social workers being open in their professional environment about their lifestyle. It also is applicable to other helping professionals. The openly lesbian or gay social worker provides a positive role model for lesbian and gay clients, serves as a resource on gay and lesbian issues, effectively enhances the capability of the social service system to provide service to gay and lesbian clients, and can be a strong advocate for the eradication of homophobia in the profession and in society. The conceptual framework itself is useful for the helping person in understanding the continuous development of identity experienced by most lesbian and gay persons—including our clients.

Other chapters speak to client-worker-administrative concerns. Goodman offers specific guidelines to facilitate client-worker interaction and self-actualization, and provides ideas for a checklist for agency practice. Hidalgo focuses on administrative, personnel, and professional policies as these affect social workers' capacity for development as helping persons.

In summary, we as helping professionals have a mandate to continue our learning and attitude assessment in order to fulfill the dual goals of helping clients to be self-actualizing and facilitating societal change that will end oppression of all people. It is only as each of us develops and learns as a competent helping person that we can assure that each client and society as a whole will continue to be self-actualizing and a growth force for this and future generations. As Bernice Goodman wrote, "Difference is the essence of human civilization. It is delicate in expression. It is persistent in its survival. It is felt in all aspects of life. It is ours for the understanding. It is time for us to understand."[4]

---

[4] Bernice Goodman, *The Lesbian: A Celebration of Difference* (Brooklyn, N.Y.: Out & Out Books, 1977), p. 29.

# Glossary

This Glossary is intended to orient the reader to the more commonly used vocabulary in lesbian and gay literature and speech. It should be recognized that, as with any unique subpopulation—particularly oppressed groups—there is a constantly changing argot. Usage may also vary with generation, area of the country, socioeconomic status, or cultural background.

The definitions of terms associated with sexual orientation represent the current state of social scientific research and are commonly used by social and behavioral scientists who specialize in this area. Although the definitions represent general suggestions for usage, they may not meet the requirements of every situation. Although the terms as defined indicate generally acceptable labels for types of behavior, it must be stressed that they are labels and nothing more. The behavior and identities of real people, needless to say, vary according to circumstances, stages of life, and other situations.

**Terms Correctly Associated with Sexual Orientation**

SEXUAL ORIENTATION. The commonly accepted, scientific term for the direction of sexual attraction, emotional and/or physical attraction, and its expression. Examples of *sexual orientation*, discussed below, are *heterosexuality*, *homosexuality*, and *bisexuality*.

*Usage:* The term, *sexual preference*, is often used to express the meaning of sexual orientation. However, *sexual preference* is also often misinterpreted to mean that sexual attraction, including same-sex attraction, is generally a matter of conscious choice. Although such a choice might be possible, current research indicates that sexual orientation may not be a matter of choice. *Sexual orientation* is, therefore, the more accurate term.

Most of the material in this Glossary has been adapted from Ellen Lewin, William Paul, and Leroy S. Walker, "A Glossary of Terms Commonly Associated with Sexual Orientation" (Sacramento: Sexual Orientation Project, California State Personnel Board, September 1980).

HETEROSEXUALITY. Sexual attraction, emotion, and/or physical attraction and behavior that are primarily directed to persons of the other gender.

HOMOSEXUALITY. Sexual attraction, emotion, and/or physical attraction and behavior that are primarily directed to persons of the same gender. Other terms used to describe persons of this sexual orientation include *gay* and *lesbian*.

BISEXUALITY. Sexual attraction, emotion, and/or physical attraction and behavior that are directed to persons of both genders.

*Usage: Except for strictly scientific or scholarly uses, it is inappropriate to apply the terms heterosexual, homosexual, and bisexual* to people. Incorrectly used, these terms can be taken to indicate that sexual orientation is the sole basis of personal or group identity.

For example, a homosexual person may have ethnic, gender, geographical, political, professional, and religious identities, in addition to his or her sexual identity. The term, *homosexual,* has been popularly misinterpreted as applying only to men, and is also inappropriate because of its formal, clinical tone. Therefore, it is generally advisable to use, when possible, the terms *gay* and/or *lesbian,* instead, in referring to people of homosexual orientation.

GAY. A person whose homosexual orientation is self-defined, affirmed, or acknowledged as such. Gay also refers to homosexually oriented ideas, communities, or varieties of cultural expression (e.g., styles, lifestyles, literature, or values). The term can include bisexuals and can refer to both men and women. See also LESBIAN.

LESBIAN. A woman whose homosexual orientation is self-defined, affirmed, or acknowledged as such. *Lesbian* also refers to female homosexually oriented (and can refer to women-oriented) ideas, communities, or varieties of cultural expression (e.g., styles, life-styles, literature, or values). The term *lesbian* or *gay* usually indicates a personal or social identity, normally suggesting that the person has identified herself or himself as *lesbian* or *gay,* or that a group accepts or affirms the identification. The terms are not necessarily synonymous with *homosexual* in that a person can be homosexual or have engaged in homosexual activities without necessarily identifying as *lesbian* or *gay.* These latter terms have cultural and social connotations in addition to the sexual ones. A lesbian or gay person sees herself or himself as homosexually oriented among other sources of identity. Research indicates that *gay* is a very old term for persons of homosexual orientation and is itself older than the term *homosexual.* The term *lesbian* historically refers to the island of Lesbos where a noted poet, Sappho, and her female followers lived in the sixth century B.C.

*Usage:* As indicated, the term *gay* can refer to men and women with a homosexual orientation, and some women accept and use the term. However, some women prefer the term *lesbian* because of its clear reference to women only. Therefore, for practical purposes and for clarity, it is generally advisable, when possible, to use the term *lesbian* when referring to homosexual women; to use the term *gay* when referring to homosexual men; and to use the terms *gay* and *lesbian* or *lesbians* and *gay men* when referring to both genders. Such terms as *gay people* and *gay community* are often used to refer to both women and men of homosexual orientation. WOMEN-IDENTIFIED WOMEN. Women who have strong emotional ties and associations with other women and who seek women as the most important members of their personal support system.

**Negative Terms Associated with Sexual Orientation**

Terms like *dyke, fag,* and *queer* are sometimes used, often unintentionally, to refer to lesbians and gay men in negative terms and are equivalent to hate terms and epithets used against racial and ethnic minorities. There is a "political" usage of such words as *dyke, faggot, maricón,* or *maricona* (Spanish) by some gays and lesbians who, in a reclamation process, redefine and use with pride words formerly used as pejorative. However, because these words still carry a negative connotation in society, their positive usage is restricted to political lesbians and gay men active in the reclamation struggle.

**Popular and Miscellaneous Terms**

CLOSET, OUT OF THE CLOSET, COMING OUT, AND RELATED TERMS. Terms used to denote varying degrees of acknowledgment to others of homosexuality or bisexuality. *Out of the closet* and similar expressions also refer to dimensions of self-acceptance of homosexuality and affirmation of gay identity. HOMOPHOBIA. A term developed by behavioral scientists to describe varying degrees of fear, dislike, and hatred of homosexuals or homosexuality. Such feelings may result in prejudice, discrimination, and hostile behavior toward people believed to be homosexual.

**Graphic Symbols**  LAMBDA (λ). The eleventh letter of the Greek alphabet, the *lambda* is used by many gay men and lesbians as a symbol that identifies their sexual orientation and lifestyles. Some lesbian/gay organizations use Lambda in their name.

PINK TRIANGLE. In Nazi Germany, homosexuals were forced to wear pink triangles and were treated as the lowest of the low by the Nazis. Gay men and lesbians have reclaimed the pink triangle and wear it as a badge of honor and also as a symbol of militancy against institutionalized oppression and denial of their civil rights in the society.

INTERTWINED MALE GENETIC SYMBOL. Identifies gay men.

INTERTWINED FEMALE GENETIC SYMBOL. Identifies lesbians.

LABRYO. A sacred double ax used by the Amazons and reclaimed by modern radical lesbian feminists as their symbol.

# SECTION I

## Populations
## at Risk

---

## Interventive
## Strategies

# Introduction
## Natalie Jane Woodman

It is estimated that a minimum of 10 percent of the population are homosexually oriented. Lesbians and gays are members of every race, religion, socioeconomic, and ethnic group in American society. For each homosexual person, a minimum of three significant others are affected in a meaningful way by that lesbian or gay individual. This resource manual, therefore, is related to issues that affect at least 40 percent of the population.

It must be remembered, however, that there are as many gay lifestyles as there are gays, and any number of lesbian and gay communities, differentiated by age, class, ethnicity, common life goals, sexual interests, and gender. It should be recognized, therefore, that some problem areas may be of more concern to one group than to another and that as a result, the knowledge and skills mastered must be always considered in the light of the specific client and the problem for which help is being sought.

In the first section of the manual, materials have been informally arranged in three subsections to provide continuity and order. These groupings are (1) specific populations seen by social workers; (2) issues of concern to gay and lesbian clients—these include health issues, legal issues, and substance abuse—and (3) factors influencing interventions, as well as such interventive modalities as crisis intervention, social growth groups, and residential treatment as it affects adolescents.

# Third World
## Hilda Hidalgo

**Introduction** *Third World* is an umbrella term that includes blacks, His-
panics, Chicanos, Puerto Ricans, Native Americans, and
Asian Americans. The term is so broad that few generalizations can be made; however, the following generalizations
can be supported:

1. At least 10 percent of the population in each minority subgroup is gay/lesbian.

2. Third World lesbians/gays are victims of multiple
levels of oppression including oppression from their own
minority community.

3. Racism and classism within the gay/lesbian community are stumbling blocks to the interaction and cooperation between Third World gays/lesbians and non–Third
World gays/lesbians.

4. Third World lesbians/gays are beginning to organize
politically, using as their organizational focus their lifestyle and their Third World identity. These organizations exist at the national, regional, and local levels.

5. Cultural and class differences among Third World
lesbians/gays are significant and important in understanding the individuals included in this "identification
label." These cultural and class differences also play an
important part in the behaviors and actions taken by
a specific collective group or organization of Third World
lesbians and gays.

**Issues and** In spite of the progress made in race relations in the last
**Problems** two decades, racism remains a cornerstone of American society. Whatever issue, situation, or activity we engage in, the
Third World person must process the issue, situation, or activity from the perspective of their Third World status. For example, in addition to the problems and issues outlined in
Grace's chapter on coming out, coming out on the job could

14

include considerations such as being the only black, Asian, Puerto Rican, or other minority person in the agency; or being the one with the least seniority; or fear of being rejected by the only one or two other Third World persons on the staff; and so on. When asked to join organizational or political efforts of non–Third World gay/lesbian groups, the minority person may have the feeling of being asked as a token to legitimize efforts that will result in little or no benefit to his/her community, which is a special issue for the Third World person. As one minority group is set to compete with other minorities for the few and shrinking "minority slots," cooperation and coalition will be harder to achieve.

Politically aware Third World lesbians and gays have many demands made on them to become involved in organizations and activities. They are likely to be overextended. Unlike their non–Third World counterparts, Third World lesbians/gays can find it difficult, if not impossible, to devote all or a major portion of their energies to lesbian and gay issues and concerns. They might subordinate the lesbian/gay issue of oppression to fighting oppression based on race or ethnicity. Being overextended, they may have difficulties meeting deadlines, or because of priorities in commitments might default in following through on a previously agreed-to task (giving first attention to a crisis or issue that subsequently developed and was related to the Third World community). These actions can be misinterpreted by non–Third World persons as lack of interest, lack of responsibility, and so on. They also might negatively affect working relationships with non–Third World groups.

When involved in lesbian and gay issues, Third World individuals might prefer to be active in one of the national, regional, or local organizations sponsored by their own ethnic groups or by combined Third World groups. Having support and identification with their own groups can facilitate engaging in cooperative efforts and coalitions with non–Third World lesbian and gay organizations. In addition, these Third World groups can be valuable resources for social workers who serve Third World gay/lesbian clients. Like Third World individuals, Third World organizations often operate on limited budgets and command limited resources. Social workers making requests of these groups should be sensitive to these limitations. At the same time, the social worker should make sure that his or her behavior does not reflect a patronizing attitude. Despite financial limitations, Third World resources can provide peer support and a community for the Third World lesbian/gay client; expertise in educating agency staff on issues relating to the Third World; political and organizational muscle to agreed-upon goals and specific projects; and so on. A major problem, especially for the nonlesbian/nongay person or for the closet lesbian/gay, is locating and making initial contact with the Third World lesbian/gay group or organization. A few examples and a listing of such groups are included in the Resources section of this manual. Some "detective work" on the part of the social worker may be required because addresses and organizations change.

Finally, cultural and class differences among Third World lesbians and gays are of significance and are important in understanding the behavior of individuals and groups. Fortunately, there is information available about these factors in the literature (see References by Content Area), and the social worker can become familiar with what has been written in this area. Such knowledge can serve as a background in increasing our understanding of the Third World lesbian/gay person.

# Lesbian and Gay Adolescents
## Sue Kaplan and Sue Saperstein

It is still extremely difficult for gay/lesbian adolescents to gain acceptance or support from family or peers for their feelings and emerging identities. Although the lesbian- and gay-identifed adult is presumably independent to pursue her or his lifestyle, the lesbian or gay adolescent, as a minor, is in a very different position. The homophobic nature of school, peers, family, and traditional morality makes it difficult for the adolescent to explore alternative sexualities. Although adolescence is a period during which the young person experiences internal growth and self-development, same-sex feelings are not supported by external societal systems.

Gay and lesbian youth are as diverse as the lesbian and gay adult population. They cut across all racial, class, religious, and cultural lines and demonstrate the same degree of variance regarding the age of sexual self-awareness as all adolescent youth. Contrary to commonly accepted norms, not all gay male adolescents are effeminate, nor are all lesbians tomboys. It should, therefore, be understood that young people's sexual identity comes from internal emotions, not from stereotypical appearances.

There are a number of issues that need to be considered by social workers in order to understand lesbian and gay clients. Being a lesbian or gay adolescent is a highly problematic situation, although not all such youth experience "problems." Although some adolescents will perceive same-sex feelings, others will not, and lesbian and gay sexuality should not be viewed as immutable nor as "just a phase." In addition, "coming out" or accepting the awareness of same-sex feelings is most often a confused and chaotic process.

Because positive role models are not readily accessible to gay and lesbian children and youth, the experience of being same-sex oriented is often perceived only from a negative viewpoint. Operating with no support systems, lesbian or gay adolescents usually are isolated, whether they disclose same-sex feelings or keep them hidden. This isolation contributes to internalized homophobia that may manifest itself

**17**

as repressed feelings, withdrawal, depression, and overcompensation. These emotions and actions often result in drug or alcohol abuse, poor school performance, running away, and other acting-out behavior. Oppression by those closest to the adolescent also may precipitate any of the foregoing problems for the young person and sometimes even culminates in suicidal attempts or death.

**Interventive Strategies** There are several areas where intervention is recommended in order to facilitate a positive lesbian or gay sexual identity. In the diagnostic process, it is imperative that social workers and family therapists begin to include lesbian, gay, and undefined sexual identities in their checklist of situations causing crises. Nonjudgmental attitudes must be communicated in the client-therapist interaction. The inclusion of young gay and lesbian issues in therapy is crucial because it provides a supportive educational perspective within the agency setting. It is critical that lesbian and gay adolescents who have been incarcerated because of their sexuality receive non-biased diagnosis, placement, and treatment.

Most important, service providers need to pay attention to the "coming-out" process as it may be a cause of acting-out behavior, for example, truancy or homelessness. Many adolescents struggle with the conflict of whether or not to come out. The adolescent is essentially seeking positive family and peer feedback and at the same time is fearful of alienating her or his support systems. Since lesbian and gay adolescents may exhibit hostile and defiant behavior because of their oppression, social workers need to understand the source of this behavior and channel it into positive and resourceful avenues. By supporting family communication and family intactness, social workers can help prevent gay and lesbian adolescents from being victims of homophobia. Social workers should not blame or try to find "cause" for adolescent gayness within the family. Both the adolescent and the family need to be supported and educated. The emphasis on support and acceptance obviously is even more necessary if the teenager is in crisis.

All service providers need to feel comfortable with their own sexuality as well as with the concept of adolescent sexuality in order to be effective with this population. This comfort level applies not only to one's sexual orientation but to sexual activity in general. Adolescents, too, may experience sexual excitation/arousal, and it may be in the context of same-sex fantasies or encounters. Yet, adolescents may be lacking in knowledge about how to engage in *responsible* sexual activity.[1] Because it is difficult for teenagers to speak comfortably about sexuality (that is, feelings and labels, as well as activity), a counselor's modeling behavior is crucial. Gay and nongay counselors need to be able to ask directly about heterosexuality, lesbian or gay sexuality, or bisexuality. Direct, open, frank questions communicate trust, acceptance, and protection. Because teenagers resent labeling, it is more fruitful to ask questions such as, Do you like *(girls) or (boys)*? Do you have a crush on *(Joe) or (Carol)*? At the same time, it is important for the worker to reassure the adolescent and explain the purpose in asking the questions. It is also necessary that the worker have some knowledge about the legal rights of minors and homosexuals.

Because of the learning that comes from positive role modeling, social workers should be educated and sensitized to the needs of and resources for this population. Because peer support is critical, lesbian and gay adolescents should be helped to meet others like themselves. Resources for social workers to use as supports for a positive lesbian and gay identity exist in a variety of areas. Young clients and their families should be informed about and encouraged to participate in groups such as Parents of Gays and Gays Under 21. In locations where these groups do not exist, social workers and other helping professionals might consider formation and sponsorship of such resources. Contacts with colleagues in diverse practice settings can facilitate identification of potential group members. If all else fails, Alyson Publications has instituted a process for linking "pen pals" in order to alleviate feelings of isolation.[2] Speakers' bureaus and gay/lesbian "hotlines" may also be used to find local support systems. Panels of speakers may be provided for staff training, and gay switchboards are a mechanism for information and referral to lesbian and gay services. Social workers must be in touch with political and legal events as well as gay culture in order to understand the context of their young clients' lives. If there

ing professional should find out what kinds of activities are available that match the young client's interests (e.g., sports groups, a chorus or band, an art group). Preliminary contact will set to rest fears based on myths that such contact will be "bad" for youth. Reality is that the positive role modeling that occurs will be highly beneficial.

In summary, the adolescent who is seen by a helping professional very much needs to be considered as a total person dealing with societal oppression and able to grow as a self-accepting lesbian or gay person.

**Notes**     1. Charles Silverstein and Edmund White, *The Joy of Gay Sex* (New York: Simon & Schuster, 1978); and Emily L. Sisley and Bertha Harris, *The Joy of Lesbian Sex* (New York: Simon & Schuster, 1978), can be useful resources for the social worker and his/her clients. See also "Gay Health Issues" and "Sexually Transmitted Diseases" in this manual.

2. See Ann Heron, ed., *One Teenager in 10* (Boston: Alyson Publications, 1983), pp. 115–116. These "writings by gay and lesbian youth" reveal the joy and pain of coming out and the anger at our oppressive society. They are contemporary and a good resource for "bibliotherapy" with adolescents.

# Parents of Lesbians and Gays: Concerns and Intervention
## Natalie Jane Woodman

The social worker's interventive skills may be called into play in two ways when dealing with parents whose children self-identify or are identified as lesbian/gay. First, we may be concerned with the child/adolescent/adult who is questioning whether, when, where, or how to "come out" to parents. Second, it is not unusual for parents to need outside help in coping with "new" knowledge about a child's sexual orientation (see letters later in this section).

In the first instance, it is not unusual to hear a gay male or lesbian maintain that "it would just kill my parents if they ever found out," and sometimes this is highly realistic (e.g., if the parent is elderly, has a serious illness, and is rigidly opposed to homosexuality). Another common assertion is "I know that I'll lose my parents forever if I came out to them," and the costs of such loss may be so great as to totally outweigh any benefits. Conversely, many lesbians and gays recognize that it is necessary to have a closer relationship with parents and that withholding a part of oneself is impeding this closeness; that it is highly possible that parents will find out from some other person, particularly if one is becoming more active or visible in the lesbian/gay community; or that parents already have a fairly good idea about the situation but are not broaching the subject openly.

For the parents themselves, help is often sought in dealing with guilt, anger, concerns for a child's happiness in the years to come, religious issues, and any of the myriad of myths that are part of the parents' own homophobic socialization. The parents may also lack basic information about sexual orientation and lesbian and gay lifestyles. They may seek help just to know what questions to ask their child.

**Issues and Problem Areas**

---

This chapter was adapted by Natalie Jane Woodman from material developed by E. Sue Blume and the National Federation of Parents and Friends of Gays.

21

**Interventive Strategies**  With the gay or lesbian client who is considering coming out to parents, it is very necessary to weigh the pros and cons of such disclosure. The individual's own "gut level" feelings should not be underestimated, but these feelings should be explored to assess the degree to which they may be overly optimistic or a projection of continued internalized negative feelings about the individual's own identity. The social worker may then wish to use the following "No Magic Answer List" compiled by the National Federation of Parents and Friends of Gays.

*How can I tell my parents that I'm gay?*

1. First, a lot depends on how you feel about being gay. If you are comfortable with it, that helps. If you are enthusiastic about your life opportunities, that helps even further.

2. Choose the time to tell sensibly—when things are going well, or at least a certain amount of calm prevails.

3. Don't blurt it out during an argument; it will become a weapon instead of a sharing.

4. You may want to tell only your mother, or only your father (depending on your particular relationship with either).

5. Lead into the telling, if you can, with an expression of your love and concern for your parents. If you don't usually say these things, think up something nice or thoughtful to do or say.

6. Be prepared for the likelihood that the news will upset and hurt your parents, and that one or both of them may lash out at you. Try not to respond defensively and angrily, but "allow" them this initial reaction.

7. Tell them: "You loved me before you knew this. I'm still the same person I was, and I hope you still love me."

8. Keep the lines of communication open, and remember that your parents are having to change their concept of you and your life—and that they probably don't have an accurate picture of what homosexuality is.

9. Read some books on the subject, and make them available to your parents.

10. If they cannot deal with this subject rationally, don't force the issue. Don't flaunt yourself or your friends defiantly—but if your parents are willing to meet your friends, make sure that they have the chance to do so.

11. Remember how long it took you to come to terms with your sexual preference and then how long it took you to get to the point of talking to your parents. So, when they can't seem to "understand" right away, be sure to give them time to take in all this new information.

Finally, the worker should be aware of readings to recommend to clients and parents (see References by Content Area) and should verbalize his or her availability to all for any future help in the communication process. Support during this time may avoid later hostilities or recriminations from either the lesbian/gay child or from parents.

The following letter appeared in a Bay Shore, New York, **Working** newspaper. The response, prepared by E. Sue Blume, may **with Parents** prove useful in working with parents with similar concerns.[1]

Dear Open Mind:

I recently learned something about my 22 year old son that has hurt me very much. He came home from college with his roommate, a male, for the weekend.

One night he confided in me that he is gay and he and his roommate are lovers. I am heartsick over this. His father would kill him if he found out. Nothing like this has ever happened before in our family. Is he mentally ill? Is there a cure? I am so upset; but feel embarrassed to talk to anyone about this. What can I do?

No Name

Dear Mother of a Gay Son:

The distress which you are experiencing has been shared by many other parents who must deal with homosexuality of a son or daughter. It is the result of society's traditional attitude that homosexuals are immoral, sick, "bad" people, and the assumption that parents, particularly mothers, are to blame for this "problem" in their children.

Your son's sexual orientation is not your "fault." *You did nothing wrong.* While the origin of homosexuality (and heterosexuality, for that matter) is not known, there is no evidence that parents are in any way responsible. (See Bell, Weinberg, and Hammersmith's official Kinsey report, *Sexual Preference,* if you are interested in finding out what's wrong with all the "cause" theories.)[2] If you want to take responsibility for anything, reflect on how you contributed to the development of a young man with the courage to face his stigmatizing identity, and the capacity to love another human being; having loving feelings for persons of the same sex is not much different from how it feels to heterosexuals; this is, after all, about love.

You are not as alone as you feel, although bearing "the secret" in your family must be a great strain. That secret can also isolate you from society. Yet *25%* of all American families can expect to have a lesbian or gay child; homosexuals and their parents alone constitute around a *third* of the population. Feelings of shame and discomfort build walls that keep people apart and weaken us. These feelings are common for gays and parents.

Homosexuality is no longer considered a mental illness. In fact, a recent study found lesbians and gays to be as well adjusted as everybody else— this, in spite of the practical and psychological stresses which can accompany the identity, like those which *you* are experiencing. Most lesbians and gays live productive lives in spite of the difficulties they face and the negative attitudes and fear (commonly called *homophobia,* these attitudes parallel racism, anti-semitism, etc., but are complicated by the fact that gays and lesbians can *pass,* or hide their identities, from society, friends, even themselves) that surround them. Your son seems to be doing just that. Therefore, the question of cure is not only irrelevant (there is no sickness) but also a reflection more of your wishes than his needs, stemming from your present discomfort: When homophobia turns inward, it can lead to emotional and relationship problems.

In issuing a statement supporting the civil rights of homosexual individuals, the American Psychiatric Association stated that homosexuality "implies no impairment in judgment, stability, or reliability, or general social or vocational capabilities." Other groups that have issued similar statements include the American Medical Association, American Bar Association, National Education Association, YWCA, and a number of religious groups and municipalities. In some states, the Sodomy Laws, under which homosexual acts (as well as many heterosexual ones) were considered illegal, have been declared unconstitutional.

This is not to dismiss or minimize your feelings, the depth of your pain. Many parents, when confronted with the homosexuality of a child in whom they have invested so much, experience something similar to the stages of grief, including feelings of shock, guilt, anger, and loss, as well as shame and fear. Many of those children are going through, or have gone through, the same feelings. While it can take time, these feelings do change.

It is crucial that you try to keep open the lines of communication with your son. He is still the same person that he was before you found out. The fact that he chose to share this "secret" with you (many gays are afraid and reluctant to "come out" to parents) is evidence of his love and trust, his desire to be open with you.

Becoming educated about the subject is also vital. Such books as *A Family Matter,* by Charles Silverstein, *Now That You Know,* by Betty Fairchild and Nancy Hayward, and *Coming Out to Parents* by Mary V. Borhek have helped many parents.[3]

Perhaps the greatest resource available to you is the support and sharing of other parents. The

National Federation of Parents and Friends of Gays at (202) 726-3223 (Washington, D.C.), or the Federation of Parents and Friends of Lesbians and Gays (Parents FLAG) at (213) 472-8952 (Los Angeles, Calif.), can tell you about nearby groups which offer telephone and group assistance. You might discuss the issue of your husband with them.

If your feelings become too much of a burden, you might want to talk to a counselor or social worker as a resource. Be careful, however, to avoid those therapists who are biased against, or uneducated about, gay and lesbian cultures; they will only prolong your distress. Until recently, the various schools of therapy all promoted damaging concepts related to homosexuality, and many still hold at least some of the old ideas. Parent groups as well as local lesbian and gay hot lines can recommend someone near you.

Certainly, the views expressed in this letter are not universal: bias against homosexuality still abounds, and your pain is unfortunate testament to the damage such bias can do. Be patient, learn, and share. After all, it is not homosexuality that destroys families, but the fear, ignorance, and lack of communication that often surround it. With work and love, your family bonds can be not weakened, but strengthened. Good luck to you.

*E. Sue Blume, CSW*

**Notes**

1. The letter and an excerpt from the response were published in "Open Mind," *The Graphic,* May 6, 1982.

2. Alan P. Bell et al., *Sexual Preference: Its Development in Men and Women* (Bloomington: Indiana University Press, 1981).

3. Charles Silverstein, *A Family Matter: A Parent's Guide to Homosexuality* (New York: McGraw Hill Book Co., 1978); Betty Fairchild and Nancy Hayward, *Now That You Know: What Every Parent Should Know about Homosexuality* (New York: Harcourt Brace Jovanovich, 1981); and Mary V. Borhek, *Coming Out to Parents: A Two-Way Survival Guide for Lesbians and Gay Men and Their Parents* (New York: Pilgrim Press, 1983).

# The Lesbian or Gay Couple as a Family: Principles for Building Satisfying Relationships
Travis L. Peterson and
Josephine H. Stewart

Travis L. Peterson and
Josephine H. Stewart

It is hoped that the issues addressed in this chapter will assist **Introduction**
practitioners in working with lesbian and gay male couples
who come to them for help. Heterosexual and homosexual
couples have many similar characteristics and struggle with
many similar issues. The different characteristics, needs, and
pressures that are encountered in working with homosexual
couples are identified. As building and strengthening positive
relationships is of primary importance, we attempt to highlight
problem areas and identify strategies and techniques that
may prove useful in counseling.

Heterosexual society has developed rituals and sanctions that **Nature of the**
lead to the establishment of heterosexual long-term relation- **Relationship**
ships, that is, couples and families. There is a pattern for
dating and courting followed by an engagement and finally
a marriage that is a public ceremony, frequently religious
and always legal. Should the marriage dissolve, another legal
process, a divorce, is required.

### Expectations, Striving, and Values
Society puts great pressure on heterosexual couples to
conform to certain life patterns: to marry; to divide work
into that which produces income and household duties); to
carry out social roles along traditional lines; to save for and
eventually buy a house; to beget children; to maintain ties
with families of origin; to attend family, professional, and
work-related functions as a couple; and so on. However,
because such pressures are less frequent in lesbian or gay
subcultures, they may not figure in the expectations that

members of a couple have for each other. The paucity of visible models for lesbian and gay couples adds to the problem of clarity in the nature of the relationship, in expectations, and in boundaries. As Decker has stated,

> Homosexual couples have to define their roles in the relative absence of models of same-sex intimacy. Raised by heterosexual parents, lacking marriage manuals and images of conjugal bliss on film or T.V. ...gay couples have had to wing-it when it comes to creating workable love and life relationships.[1]

The absence of societal pressure or support to maintain the relationship also contributes to a couple's failure to enunciate expectations. The ever-present threat of outside sexual partners or sexual acting out (especially in the gay male community) is another factor in the lack of stability of lesbian and gay relationships.

The role many heterosexual families of origin play in establishing the "new couple" (for example, giving financial assistance) is largely missing in the case of the lesbian or gay couple. In addition, the sense of belonging, identity, sharing, and support that exist for many heterosexual couples and the role many extended family members play in helping the couple resolve conflicts or adjust to difficulties are usually absent.

First and foremost, the task of the social worker in counseling is to open lines of communication, to clarify the expectations each partner has of the other and of the relationship. This can be done by having the partners come to some clear agreements. Though the nature and wording of positive, formal contracts is so complex that the topic cannot be thoroughly addressed here, two books by Sager and by Ables may prove helpful.[2] However, it is suggested that the following areas be covered in any contract of lesbian or gay male couples:

1. A clause stating "we will be together until _____" and including circumstances that might precipitate a breakup.

2. Provision for being the other's best friend as well as lover (this addresses the basic need for honesty and openness with each other).

3. Provisions for the rights to argue, disagree, and hold differing opinions without loss of the relationship.

4. The right within the relationship to be individuals, with individual interests, outlets, idiosyncracies, and duties.

5. Clarification that the contract is between two persons who basically love themselves, are secure with themselves, and do not need another to prove their acceptability (this is intended to prevent inappropriate and unhealthy dependence and to promote interdependence).

6. Methods for resolving conflict.

7. Joint ownership of property and provision for handling finances. (This is best handled in a separate legal agreement and legal wills; see the chapter by Fern W. Schwaber in this manual.)

8. Provision for a monogamous or open sexual relationship. If the couple has agreed to an open sexual relationship, measures for handling and communicating about external interactions should be specified.

**Communicating, Solving Problems, and Resolving Conflicts**

Two ways to develop better, more open communication and facilitate problem-solving and conflict resolution skills are to help each of the partners achieve a better sense of self and use self-assertive techniques. Open communication and self-assertion principles include, but are not limited to, the following:

1. Each partner must make clear what he or she expects and wants from the other and from the relationship and how he or she wants the relationship to develop in the future (even if the answer is "I don't know"). People can make decisions and act given the facts and an honest approach. They cannot act responsibly on innuendoes and lack of information.

2. If one wants a commitment from another, he or she needs to *ask* for it rather than to *assume* that there is a commitment. Failure to keep a commitment needs to be confronted as soon after the infraction as possible.

3. When one expresses personal idiosyncracies, wishes, pet peeves, individuality, and so forth, and these are not respected by the other, then caution is advised. It is necessary to request clearly and emphatically how one wants such sharing to be received.

4. The right to have a contract and the right to have a commitment should be established, if not from the outset of the relationship, then certainly after a reasonable length of time in a loosely defined arrangement has passed. Lack of a contract or commitment will disperse the couple's energy, resources, and time to other life pursuits that are perceived as more constructive than the love relationship.

5. The right to some compromises, to differences of opinion, and to having one's feelings and opinions respected should be specified.

6. The use of "dirty names"—which blocks communication or prevents conflict resolution—should be recognized and dealt with.

7. "Time out" may be requested when an argument becomes too heated. This enables each partner to "cool down," reorganize thoughts, and come back in a more constructive, negotiating mood.

8. If one's time commitments or performances of duties are the source of disagreement, one's mate should be asked to help set priorities.

Open, honest communication is essential and minimizes the withholding of expression of feelings or the misinterpreting of the other's behaviors. Without such dialogue, the feeling of being unloved or discounted can quickly develop and anxiety about loss or the fear of abandonment will follow.

## Autonomy vs. Mutuality

Problems of independence, particularly when one partner is not as emotionally developed as the other, may lead to identity fusion. Jealousy and possessiveness are often present when there is identity fusion or when control and competition become issues for the pair. The complaint that is often presented to the social worker is that one partner makes all the decisions because of the indecisiveness of the other.

Another concern, especially seen in lesbian couples but not exclusive to them, is the *belief that one partner is responsible for the other's happiness.* This belief, that one can be responsible for another's well-being, happiness, and success, is learned dogma that must be unlearned by couples striving for equality in relationships.

### Other Problems

Other areas that create problems in both heterosexual and homosexual couples include the following: sexuality and the expression of sexuality; money—having it, lacking it, using it; and other issues stemming from differences in values, beliefs, and patterns of behavior developed over the years before the two people got together. Issues that are special to lesbians and gay men and that may be serious blocks or obstacles to building satisfying relationships or that may create added stress include the following:

1. The degree of self-acceptance and acceptance of lesbian or gay orientation that the individual has achieved; homophobia is not exclusive to heterosexuals.

2. The lack of support systems within the community and the lack of positive role models for successful homosexual couples.

3. The degree to which one partner has come out to others—to the family of origin, to nongay friends, on the job, and so forth—and the degree to which the other is closeted.

4. Unequal incomes or work status.

5. Monogamy versus open sexual relationships, and especially the degree to which maintaining friendships with exlovers causes problems in the current relationship.

6. Because many lesbians and gay men have had heterosexual marriages and children prior to the decision to live a lesbian or gay lifestyle, lesbian mothers and gay fathers bring additional demands on their emotional energy, their time, and their money into the new relationship.

The social worker has a responsibility to be attuned to these particular stresses and to use a breadth of interventive strategies in resolving problems with the couple. Various authors have addressed these areas, and useful books will be found in the References by Content Area at the end of this volume.

**Summary** Lesbian and gay male couples are viable family units that can benefit from counseling to build satisfying relationships. Social workers trained and skilled in couple counseling will quickly recognize the many similarities in counseling with heterosexual couples. Problem areas that become the focus of intervention likewise are similar. Differences come from the added stress lesbians and gay men experience in living a lifestyle that is unacceptable to the majority of society.

Practitioners who have been trained in traditional schools of social work face the need to broaden their knowledge base to include information about lesbians and gay men; their communities; the existing resources available to them; and the discrimination they face in employment, housing, educational and religious institutions, health care, and social activities. Counselors are further cautioned to do considerable soul-searching to recognize their own biases—perhaps even homophobia—as these exist in themselves, in their profession, and in the social agencies and institutions in which they practice.

**Notes**   1. Beverly Decker, "Counseling Gay and Lesbian Couples," in "Homosexuality and Social Work," double issue of *Journal of Social Work and Human Sexuality*, 2 (Winter 1983–Spring 1984), p. 41.

2. Clifford J. Sager, *Marriage Contracts and Couple Therapy* (New York: Brunner/Mazel, 1976); and Billie S. Ables, *Therapy for Couples* (San Francisco: Jossey-Bass, 1977). See also the chapter on legal issues by Kathleen Mayer in this manual.

# Lesbian Mothers
## Audrey I. Steinhorn

The U.S. Department of Labor in its most recent report indicates that almost one of every five families with children in the United States was maintained by one parent, an increase of 79 percent since 1970.[1] These figures give evidence of more flexibility of lifestyles, including lesbian motherhood. As a group, lesbian mothers are one of the least-visible and most-misunderstood minorities in our society today—yet their number is estimated to be between 5 and 15 million.[2]

Women become lesbian mothers via many different life experiences. Some women made a conscious choice to hide their homosexual identity for the sake of a more socially accepted and respected heterosexual relationship, bore children, and later were not able to continue the "straight masquerade." Other women were unaware of their lesbianism until they were married and had children. Still others made an intentional choice for parenthood, choosing artificial insemination, a planned pregnancy, or adoption.

No matter how she attained motherhood, and regardless of the quality of her parenting, a lesbian mother is singularly different from the heterosexual counterpart. She has no legal protection against having her children taken away from her solely because of her sexual orientation. In the case of lesbian mothers, society's fear of and hostility toward homosexuality affects the guarantee of basic rights such as privacy, freedom of association and speech, and equal protection under the law. The fear that she cannot be an acknowledged lesbian and still be allowed by society to keep her children, combined with the guilt she may feel for burdening her children with this difference, can be damaging to the lesbian mother's self-esteem.

An expanded version of this article appears in *Women and Therapy*, 1 (Winter 1982), pp. 35–48. © 1983 by the Haworth Press, Inc.

Few areas of living and child rearing are free from anxiety for lesbian mothers. In dealing with financial responsibilities, custody agreements, family relationships, child care arrangements, love affairs, or social relationships, they are subject to specific fears that nongay single parents cannot imagine or identify with. Disclosure of sexual identity to their children presents an even more potentially traumatic event.

## Child Support

**Interventive Issues**

The issue of requesting more child support or instituting court proceedings to collect delinquent payment often includes the broader question of Does he or doesn't he [the father of the child] know that I am a lesbian? This question can precipitate an intense panic involving many kinds of anticipated reactions and/or consequences. While it is important to differentiate rational from irrational fears, it must be noted that it is never completely irrational for a lesbian mother to fear loss of her children should her sexual and affectional orientation become known.

## Custody

The most critical encounter for a lesbian mother may be a custody battle for her children with the legal controversy based on the grounds that her lifestyle makes her an "unfit mother." In defending her sexual orientation and personal beliefs in court, the lesbian mother is in fact attempting to prove that she is not a danger to her own children and, more specifically, to her children's gender-identity development. Under the guise of concern about the impact of social stigma on the child and concern about "parental neglect" lurks society's fear that the children might be influenced by parental role modeling to "choose" to be gay. The reality is that sexual orientations of growing children cannot be predicted or "molded." However, in court, the lesbian mother is in the unique position of defending her sexual orientation not only for herself, but also for her child—of showing that she believes that if her child were to be gay, it would not be because the child has a lesbian mother.

Current research finds no reason not to support lesbian mothers simply because they differ from their nongay peers in their choices of life mates.[3] Studies also refute the negative stereotypes of lesbians and should serve to remind all social workers to be informed of current knowledge relating to lesbian issues, rather than to act on assumptions and biases they may have.

### Family Relations and Identity Disclosure

Every child needs to know about sexuality and sex, affection and love, and commitment to a relationship. The unique dimension for a lesbian is sharing with her child love for someone of the same sex. If the mother does not reveal her sexual orientation, her "secret" could create strain and conflict for all family members. The worker's sensitivity to the stresses a mother undergoes in coming out to her children is imperative.

For example, the social worker can elicit and explore various fears with the lesbian mother, such as the mother's fear of losing her children in a custody case, being rejected by her children because of her sexual orientation, and her children's being rejected by their peers because of her sexual orientation. The social worker can use his or her knowledge and skills to help the lesbian mother and significant others differentiate projections from fears that have some basis in reality. A thorough grounding in developmental stages can enable the social worker to help the mother distinguish between her projections and realistic age-appropriate responses in her children. For example, the response of an adolescent to a mother's coming out will be different from the response of a 5-year-old.

The children's knowledge of their mother's lesbianism is important to their understanding of her and is a way of sharing an important part of her world. Similarly, children will need to feel that they can talk with their mothers about how different it might be for them to be children of lesbians. This is particularly true for teenagers who are dealing with their own issues of sexuality, because they will probably not have a supportive peer group who also have lesbian or gay parents. This mutual sharing can provide the opportunity for each mother and her children to meet the difficulties along the road of growing up and achieving maturity from a stable base of knowledge and security.

## Social Relationships

Lesbian mothers who seek help need a supportive peer network as well as specific professional assistance. Social workers must be sensitive to particular problems of this group of mothers who struggle frequently with an extreme sense of isolation at being "caught between" two groups—nonparenting lesbians who may have ambivalent feelings toward motherhood and children and single heterosexual women who are heads of households who may reject lesbians because of their sexual orientation. Familiarity with the lesbian subculture and networks for parents and their children can enable social workers to be more effective with lesbian mothers.

**Conclusion**  All persons have the right to define and express their sexuality and to develop their own potential as long as they do not encroach on the rights of òthers. Social workers can provide the necessary support to lesbian mothers if we educate ourselves to the realities of homosexuality, understand our personal biases, and utilize current research. Lesbian mothers need support to be at peace with their orientation, which does not reflect the dominant culture, and we must be leaders in helping others to change their attitudes and behaviors, which are oppressive to this minority group. Concomitantly, we must help lesbian mothers to accept and believe in themselves and assist them to establish a fundamental base as lesbians for personal security and the welfare of their children.

**Notes**  1. U.S. Department of Labor, Bureau of Labor Statistics, Bulletin 2158, Washington, D.C., March 1983.

2. Nan Hunter and Nancy Polikoff, "Custody Rights of Lesbian Mothers: Legal Theory and Litigation Strategy," 25 *Buffalo L. Rev.* 691 (1976); Trial Brief for Plaintiff at 1, Stamper v. Stamper, No. 75-054-550-DM (Mich. Cir. Ct., Wayne County); and "The Avowed Lesbian Mother and Her Right to Child Custody: A Constitutional Challenge That Can No Longer Be Denied," Law Note, 12 *San Diego L. Rev.* 799, 820 (1975).

3. Richard Green, Mary Hotvedt, Jane Barclay Mandel, and Laurel Smith, "Entrance into Therapy: Presenting

Complaints of Homosexual and Heterosexual Mothers";
Beverly Hoeffer, "Children's Sex-Role Learning in Lesbian
Mother Families"; and Ellen Lewin and Terrie A. Lyons,
"Divorce and Coming Out: Maturational Crises," papers
presented at Panel 152, "Lesbian Mothers and Their Families:
Implications for Research and Clinical Practice," American
Orthopsychiatric Association Meeting, Toronto, Ont., Canada,
April 1980.

# People Who Are Gay or Lesbian and Disabled
## Kirby Wohlander and Marla A. Petal

**P**roviding social work services to gay or lesbian clients with a disability requires awareness of and sensitivity to issues relating to disability, disability and sexuality, and the exercising of sexual options. About one out of every ten persons in the United States is disabled and the estimate that one out of every ten persons is gay would mean that there are at least three million people who are both gay and disabled. There is a great need for sensitive, educated social workers for this population, especially gay and lesbian counselors. It is incumbent upon those of us who do not understand from personal experience the unique dynamics of being lesbian or gay and disabled to educate ourselves.

A disability may be in hearing, vision, mobility, mental abilities, or otherwise related to physical or mental functioning. Every individual with a disability is a person whose uniqueness may be significantly affected by the type of disability, age of onset, educational experience, parental acceptance and overprotection, and so on. The collective experience of people who are both gay or lesbian and disabled is only a collection of very particular individual struggles. The authors depart radically from the medical model's view of the problem as one of deviance or dysfunction and instead view the issue in terms of the physical and attitudinal barriers created and perpetuated in the social environment.

The disability rights movement, which has grown in recent years, has had far-reaching influence on government,

The authors gratefully acknowledge the comments and resources provided by Barbara Waxman, Don Kilhefner, Neal Twyford, Gary Sanderson, and the men of the gay disabled support group, Community Service Center for the Disabled, San Diego, Calif.

institutions, and individuals. The essential value expressed by this movement is that people with disabilities should have the same rights as those who are not disabled, and should not be limited by denial of self-determination, access to public places, usable transportation, access to mass communications and media, equal opportunity in educational and vocational pursuits, or other aspects of daily living. In other words, the freedom to participate in the joys and responsibilities of community life is essential. One of these basic human rights is the right to be accepted as sexual beings, responsible for making one's own choices about behaviors, partners, and children, and to be informed and to have access to needed services in this area.

The myths that have grown around the area of sexuality and disability are pervasive. It is important that we recognize these sexually oppressive myths in all their subtle forms.

**Attitudinal Barriers and Intervention**

The myth that people with a disability are dependent, childlike, and need to be protected has as a corollary that disabled people are asexual. The medical model has taught us to see people with disabilities as "patients." A potent implication of this role is that a disabled person's major life decisions may be made by others—doctors, family members, professionals.

Following the mistaken assumptions that individuals with a disability cannot participate fully in life, and are not quite whole human beings, are the equally paternalistic and wrong notions that people with disabilities are sexually undesirable, sexually inadequate, and—one hopes—lack sexual feelings too. A not surprising consequence of this is the tendency to limit the range of truly acceptable sexual expression. Many people with a disability have taken on the beliefs of their oppressors and have learned to discount and suppress their sexuality. As one person has expressed it, "The hope is that disabled people will choose to just miss out on sex because it would be too difficult and no partners would be available anyway."

Gay and lesbian people and people with disabilities have frequently experienced similar frustrations at the hands of professionals who do not see them in the framework of normal human expression and view them as pathological in relation to the degree of their divergence from "normal" lifestyles. The shallow myth that individuals who opt for a homosexual lifestyle do so because of some inability to succeed sexually in a predominantly heterosexual society is easily and quickly applied to people with a disability. Such conclusions are clearly offensive to self-determined, self-confident gay and lesbian people. For some people, the experience of dealing with oppression in one area of their lives makes it easier to cope with and overcome it in another. For others, one oppression simply complicates the other.

Our culture promotes rigid and stereotypic physical images of sexual desirability. Sexuality is merchandized and removed from emotional factors and choice of partners. Orgasm is generally viewed as the goal of sexual intercourse and essential to sexual satisfaction. These limitations on sexual expression are extremely oppressive to people with disabilities, no less in the gay community than among heterosexuals. Thus for many people with a disability who have chosen a gay lifestyle, the predominant experience in the gay community is one of isolation. Although some disabilities may affect the capacity to achieve orgasm or maintain erection, social workers should know that this need not be regarded as a limitation in ultimate ability to experience or provide sexual satisfaction.

Inasmuch as the assumption is made that disabled people are sexually undesirable, then nondisabled partners are suspected of pathology and of being unable to attract anyone else. This devaluation by association extends the stigma of disability to those who may be challenging that myth.

Another myth is that disability breeds disability. A measure of our society's generalized fear of the sexuality of people with disabilities is the horror that greets a mentally retarded couple's decision to marry. Ironically, the fear that people with disabilities will have children has led some to view homosexual expression as less threatening. Though not unrelated, it would require a separate discussion to examine the links between sexual oppression, denial of reproductive rights, eugenics, and disability. A classic example is the fact that 350,000 people with disabilities underwent forced sterilization under the Nazis.

Disabled people have, in many cases, been denied sex

education as a result of these prejudices. Established programs have failed to make themselves available and responsive to the needs of people with disabilities. As the channels for learning sexual behaviors are cut off, sexual fulfillment becomes less attainable. Many people who have grown up in a vacuum of knowledge about sexuality, about their own disabilities, and about their bodies may have filled the gaps with mistaken assumptions.

The specific consequences of various disabilities can be very different. For example, the experience of someone who has an adventitious disability such as traumatic spinal cord injury (most frequently associated with sports or driving accidents in young men) is different from the experience of the congenitally disabled person. Not only must these individuals cope with the devastating impact of injury on every major aspect of their lives, but also with their fears about their inability to fulfill previously held sexual expectations. Problems in sexual functioning begin to cloud everything else. Although the best rehabilitation centers confront the issue almost immediately, some continue to treat it as taboo or too controversial to deal with.

Adults who are mentally retarded frequently carry learned dependence and low self-esteem into sexual encounters and may allow themselves to be used. For people who are visually impaired, the central problems revolve around achieving a sense of privacy. Visual impairment also inhibits the search for information and complicates the process of coming out as a gay person. Communication, both in access to information and between partners, is the central problem for people who have a hearing impairment.

The discrimination experienced by gay and lesbian people with disabilities is threefold: homophobia among peers in the disabled community, devaluation and denial of potential in the gay community, and some of each from the able-bodied, straight world. As a first step, social workers must recognize every individual's right to be viewed as a sexual being. It is incumbent on the counselor to assume little and to facilitate the client's discovery and expression of his or her potential. The social worker is required to believe in and practice basic principles and skills; to be sensitive, caring, accepting, and open; and to allow clients to choose options congruent with their own values, attitudes, capabilities, and desires.

It is important for the social worker to have or learn a basic understanding of the client's disability. Social work practitioners must at the outset confront their own emotional responses to disability and the stereotypes they hold. It is people with disabilities who themselves are best able to eliminate our prejudices and fears. Nor should gay and lesbian counseling centers shirk the responsibility to learn to serve this population, with the assistance of local independent living centers.

## Physical Barriers and Intervention

The right to be informed and have access to needed services and the right to explore one's individual potential require physical and programmatic modifications of the gay community environment. Agencies providing counseling and health services, as well as the organizations, activities, and meeting places of the gay community, should examine their facilities, policies, and programs to identify the barriers that prevent equal access to people with disabilities.

The solutions are not very complicated. Local independent living centers will often assist in evaluating accessibility and provide technical information about the following: designated handicapped parking, curb cuts at corners, ramps into buildings, elevators, modified rest rooms (widened doors, stalls, grab bars, etc.), lowered water fountains, easy-open doors, widened doors, audio crosswalk signals, thermoform maps, raised letter and brailled signs, cassette-taped and brailled materials, certified sign-language interpreters (for counseling, meetings, concerts, etc.), telecommunication devices for the deaf (compatible with telephone systems), telephone handset amplifiers, captioning on films, informational signs, sign-language classes, adapting written materials and specially prepared materials, accessibility symbols for use on public relations materials, and so on.

These simple measures often require a small outlay of money and a larger one of advocacy. The process of sensitizing ourselves to creating a barrier-free environment is a major and a first step in diminishing attitudinal barriers. It is people with disabilities themselves who will educate us to overcome prejudice and fear.

# Social Service Needs and Resources in Rural Communities
## Breeze

For the past four years, I have resided in a rural community comprised of ten small towns ranging in population from about four hundred to nine thousand. Each town has its own identity, yet the majority of them are predominantly conservative, traditional, and fundamentalist—maintaining the "Old West" frontier mentality. When I moved to this rural area as the director of a new social service agency, my early paranoia of being "discovered" as a lesbian was somewhat lessened. Maybe it was age; maybe it was the fact that one of the ten communities had gays openly living there; and maybe it was the fact that I was new to the area and had no primary relationship at the time. Gradually I learned that there are many gays and lesbians living in all these towns—living in secrecy with few or no support systems available to them.

The agency I administered provided general social services offering a variety of programs, specializing in information and referrals, and promoting client advocacy. I started a twenty-four-hour crisis line shortly after we opened, yet we had only two calls related to gay/lesbian issues within the first fifteen months. There was also an established mental health clinic serving the ten communities, and it also has seen relatively few gay clients. This organization had made no special outreach efforts to the lesbian and gay members of the area. The lesbian/gay clients the clinic has seen came with problems other than those related to being gay in an isolated community. Because the clinic has no therapists that are gay/lesbian, personnel are unaware of the differing experiences of the gay population and see no need for special services.

**Isolation** To illustrate this further, let me cite some examples. A lesbian who teaches at one of the high schools had bought land in a neighboring small town and planned to build a house for herself. However, when a neighbor threatened to reveal the teacher's sexual orientation to the school administration, she abandoned her plans. Several female students have sent the teacher love notes, which only exacerbates her constant fear of discovery. Another lesbian moved away from one of the communities because she knew of no other lesbians there. Even with her partner, she felt totally isolated and tired of living a life of secrecy. The couple used to drive fifty miles to a rural college town once a week just to meet with other lesbians in a support group. When they met some lesbians from a town adjoining theirs, they not only left the group, but had an added impetus for the move away from the area. One of my former employees found out that I was a lesbian shortly after I hired her. Difficulties in work relationships quickly developed, and when she left, she wrote a note for me stating that working with a feminist lesbian was more than she could bear (and she was a former welfare rights worker!).

I have met or heard about many lesbians and gay men in each of our towns, yet many of them don't know about each other and live in total isolation. There are no means of communication or support systems, no organized social activities, no special counseling services, no bars, and no gathering places exclusively for lesbians and gays. For young persons growing up in a rural area such as ours, there are no visible role models in their world. They suffer a perpetual identity crisis for lack of anyone to talk with about their sexual orientation.

Youth and single gays and lesbians in rural areas may be particularly vulnerable to crises related to identity confusion. They are deprived of any nonstereotypic educational materials because of school and library censorship. As a result, the only exposure to homosexuality is from the media (therefore stereotypic), from the churches (that it is sinful), or from peers (that such people are crazy or sexually inadequate). Thus they feel forced into leading a pseudoidentity. Some reluctantly date people of the opposite sex rather than have no social life at all and may try hard to "become straight" in order to have a sexually intimate relationship. The individual's self-concept, however well integrated, becomes distorted when no supports exist.

Along with the lack of educational materials, there is frequent repression of any open discussion about homosexuality. Few people feel free to ask questions about this taboo subject, and fewer yet are willing to share factual information and resources to raise people's consciousness.

Another major lack for gays and lesbians in rural communities is legal assistance. There is not one attorney in these ten communities sympathetic to gay or feminist issues. In fact, I have had three lesbians request assistance on three separate issues that were probably related to their being gay, yet I had no proof of discrimination and no legal expertise to assist them. One lost a job in the private sector, one was arrested for a barroom brawl (a rare charge against men in this particular town), and one was physically abused by a police officer and had her car damaged on the suspicion that she was "fleeing from arrest." Although she was acquitted of the charge of "fleeing from an officer," no compensation has been awarded, no investigation of the officer has occurred, and no attorney will take her case. These are typical problems for all minorities in rural communities, but gays and lesbians are the least likely to be given any assistance by the legal services agency for poor people. The state Civil Liberties Union states that they need strong evidence that harassment occurs because the client is lesbian/gay—a difficult fact to prove. My own legal involvement in behalf of these lesbian clients occurred without encouragement from my agency's board of directors. Thus, lesbian and gay legal rights in rural communities are usually fought in isolation and without community support.

**Legal Assistance**

There are some unique countercultural small towns where lesbians are freely open and where individual privacy is a prized possession. When social contact is desired, members of the group congregate informally. Gay men in one town remain isolated and in a numerical minority. Yet in another

**Networking**

town, the gay males are more open, perhaps because it is a resort community. However, neither group displays any interest in organizing with others. Their needs are met by their own social network. This apathy and separatism are a hindrance to other lesbians and gays who are hidden in the more traditional towns, do not know how to make contact, and may actually fear being seen with those lesbians and gays who do not hide their sexual preference.

Shortly after my arrival in this rural area, I thought about what could be done to develop some kind of gay network. I inquired about a lesbian rap group in the rural college town previously mentioned and discovered it was initiated by the mental health clinic. It had begun as a lesbian/gay mixed group. The lesbians broke away to form their own feminist lesbian group and received support from the then existing women's center. The center served all women without discrimination and actively supported the lesbian group by making referrals to it and advertising it in their posters and newsletters. The center consequently received considerable harassment from the community, including some of their own membership. This took the form of lack of cooperation from the police and funding sources for about two years before their reputation as "radical lesbians" subsided. It is interesting that there were never any gays and lesbians on the staff of that women's center.

The writing of this chapter led me to thinking about approaching the mental health clinic in our area to propose that they initiate a new lesbian/gay support group for all ten communities. Because they have been here for over a decade, are fairly well respected, and represent establishment philosophies, they would probably receive some acceptance from the community. However, in a discussion with one of the therapists there, it was learned that fear of a homophobic community reaction "might present problems" should such outreach be made to gay clients. Also, this population "is not one of the priorities for the next five years." Since the clinic director has been explicit in stating to job applicants that this is a very "traditional" agency, it seems unlikely that it will attract or hire a self-identified lesbian or gay social worker in the near future. Thus, chances for coordination with the clinic appear to be nonexistent under the present administration.

Obviously, it is an arduous task to develop a support network in rural communities where networking is of vital importance. Rural resources are limited, we are more exposed and vulnerable, and our support is minimal—if it exists at all. When I heard that a statewide NASW Lesbian and Gay Task Force was being formed, I eagerly became one of its first members—and the only one outside the metropolitan area in which our meetings were held. The task force's goal for that year was to present a professional workshop on working with gay and lesbian clients. It was a remarkable success and provided our group with professional credibility in the state NASW chapter. The task force now has regular committee status on the board. Two primary objectives of that early task force were (1) public education about the needs of lesbians/gays, and (2) encouragement of profesional gays and lesbians to come out publicly in support for gay rights. The first objective was more successful than the second—for obvious reasons. Both objectives continue to be pursued.

Although I had left my agency by the time the first workshop was presented, I was still active on the Board of Directors of the Arizona State Chapter, NASW and in my community as a volunteer. Later in that year, at the NASW state conference, I copresented a paper on counseling gay and lesbian clients and discovered a service provider from another rural community was in the audience. Through her I was eventually invited to speak to a rural mental health clinic staff on working with gay and lesbian clients. Their reception was incredibly supportive.

## What Professionals Can Do

As professional social workers, we must, I believe, begin talking to other social service providers about serving the lesbian/gay population. We are the ones who can help to educate them about the problems this minority experiences. Once we enlist support, we can all develop programs that begin to meet the needs of lesbians and gays. For example, in my work with the regional office of the public assistance/foster care/child protective agency (as chair of the executive committee for in-service training), another inroad has been made. The coordinator of the foster care program, who had not thought before about the possibility of having lesbian teenagers in the program, has agreed to check this out and make referrals of any young women who may want to talk with someone.

Once we have obtained credibility as professionals, we have the opportunity to address issues that have been neglected in social programs. We can't expect others who don't understand the problems to develop adequate services. It is in our own interest—and that of our sisters and brothers—that we should lead the way. Whether we come out as gay/lesbian professionals is another matter entirely. If we are recognized as minority advocates or innovative social workers, the question of sexual orientation need not be raised. However, if we want to become role models for others who are lesbian/gay and occupational paranoia is not an issue, then coming out may be the greatest contribution one can perform in a rural community.

# Interventive Strategies and Realities in Working with Military Personnel
## Anonymous

The United States Army, Navy, and Coast Guard were established in 1775 and the Air Force in 1947. Singly and collectively, their primary concern is with the physical protection of our country. The population of the military has usually been male, with a contingent of "camp followers"—some male, but most female—who are often described in the literature as prostitutes, although they can be spouses and children. This group has been seen as providing services to the troops, that is, mental, physical, and emotional release of tension.

    The issue of homosexuality in the military was most often raised against the homosexual and homosexual behavior (to separate person and act) on the basis of moral turpitude. That is, the societal pressure to follow a generally accepted sexual ethic was thought to create the possibility of "blackmail" or covert pressure on those who did not comply with this ethic—because of practicing unacceptable sexual behavior (thereby, by implication, endangering the country). Not considered was the fact that if one is open about one's orientation and, if that orientation is accepted by an employer, blackmail is not possible. Probably another area of concern was the homophobic belief in the myth of "enticement" and "contagion." Also, in the past, to be thought to be an individual who would prefer homosexual rather than heterosexual activity, even if one did not act on this preference, was sufficient reason to label and ostracize the person. Finally, the issue of gays/lesbians in the military in the present day has changed in scope somewhat with the inclusion of an

**History and Description of the Population at Risk**

The author is an MSW in the armed services whose career would be jeopardized if anonymity were not maintained. The manual committee appreciates the efforts expended in providing this material.

49

increased number of women in the ranks. Now, the armed services must extend their concerns with "unacceptable" behavior to women as well as men. The military services continue to be the one area of federal employment excluded from the legislation prohibiting discrimination on the basis of sexual orientation. This discrimination adds to the oppression that requires secrecy for lesbian/gay personnel.

**Problem Identification** The "problem" of being lesbian or gay in the military is really no different from that in any other occupation that is rooted in the general belief system of the Christian ethic, which condemns homosexuality as sinful or immoral. This has been translated in such institutions to extend to inability to function on a job in a competent manner, thus necessitating elimination of that individual from the occupation. With the constant threat of expulsion from the service, the individual who encounters conflict during the coming out process is commonly faced with a dual identity problem— identity as lesbian/gay and identity as a service person. It would therefore follow that knowledge of the homosexual identification or sexual orientation of a member of the service will be limited to very few persons. Problem solving in areas related to sexual orientation (intra- or interpersonally) may not be sought from professional therapists because of fear of exposure. Usually, selection of a counselor is made by word-of-mouth recommendation from other people and is based on reputation in such areas as comfort level (easy to talk to), sympathetic (whether gay or not), and capacity for maintaining confidentiality. Other problem areas such as substance abuse, relationship issues, coming out to parents, or a need to discuss whether to confront the military establishment may prompt the service person to seek counseling or social work help. Sexual orientation, while not the primary focus, still is a dimension of self that cannot be denied by client or social worker. However, the social worker must beware of making sexuality the key issue. On yet another level, the individual who is "discovered" and pushed out of the closet certainly might benefit from engaging in problem solving with an accepting professional person.

Making judgments about the individual's behavior in a moralistic manner obviously is not appropriate for the professional person nor is it therapeutic for the client! When counseling is requested, it should be on a one-to-one basis unless the client clearly requests inclusion of someone else. This minimizes the risk for the individual of having another participant violate confidentiality. Keeping written notes with any labeling of behaviors is also discouraged. Often the aspect of confidentiality is crucially regulated by legality. At present, only the chaplain and legal counsel have this privilege (at this writing, the NASW Code of Ethics has not been used as a challenge within the military ranks). However, since individuals seek help from the Mental Health Center or the Community Assistance Center (both are military centers) for problems other than those associated with lesbian/gay identity issues, some other problem focus can be used for any necessary records. In summary, to protect the client, there should be no entry in records of material related to sexual orientation.

In the counseling setting, discussion of military rules and regulations can be important in clarifying the realistic consequences of overt lesbian/gay behavior. In fact, the social worker should be very open at the outset of counseling with *all* clients about his/her interpretation of professional ethics and efforts that will be made to protect confidentiality. However, individuals are usually knowledgeable about the military code of conduct. What they are looking for is a setting where there is acceptance and where they can explore alternative avenues for expression of their thoughts and feelings and find help for their behavior, sexual orientation, or other problems. Sharing information about resources available in nearby communities, in literature,[1] in legal areas,[2] and medically, in a nonjudgmental atmosphere, is a significant way to convey acceptance. It also helps the client move beyond the confines of the military setting and find needed support systems where they exist.

The interventive process for the client, then, is one of clarification, decision making, and attaining comfort for self within what continues to be an oppressive environment for lesbians and gays.

**Do's and Don'ts for Intervention**

**Notes**     1. Nancy Adair and Casey Adair, *Word Is Out: Stories of Some of Our Lives* (New York: Dell Publishing Co., 1978); A. Berube, "Coming Out Under Fire," *Mother Jones,* February/March 1983, pp. 23–29, 45; Jonathan Katz, *Gay American History: Lesbians and Gay Men in the U.S.A., a Documentary* (New York: Thomas Y. Crowell Co., 1976); and Katz, *Gay-Lesbian Almanac* (New York: Harper & Row, 1983) all contain material of historical interest to the gay or lesbian in the armed services.

2. An example of legal support systems is the State Conference Legal Defense and Education Fund of Syracuse, N.Y., which is working with Parents and Friends of Gays in the case of Air Force Lieutenant Joann Newak.

# Rewriting a Bad Script: Older Lesbians and Gays
## Raymond M. Berger

Older lesbians and gays can be the unhappiest people in the world—or the happiest. More than has been commonly assumed, it is within the power of the individual to determine his or her destiny: As one older gay man said, "We get out of life only what we put into it."

However, until the last few years, almost no reliable information about older gays and lesbians was available. While the world turned its attention to the "young warriors" of the early gay and lesbian movements, the "survivors" were overlooked. The gerontologists showed no greater interest. In fact, the now voluminous literature on the life satisfaction and social adjustment of the elderly is resoundingly silent about the 1¾ million older persons who are gay or lesbian.[1] This refusal to examine the reality of aging has occurred despite our knowledge, as early as 1948, that gays and lesbians are present in equal and substantial numbers among all age cohorts.[2] Where have the old gays and lesbians gone?

The answer is, they have been silent until now. They have **Old Script** allowed (we have *all* allowed) an incredibly false but nonetheless pervasive script to be replayed countless times in the organs of our popular culture (films, theaters, novels, and magazines) and in the theories and actions of helping professionals. The play always ends badly for the gay or lesbian character. The aging homosexual is lonely beyond human tolerance. With age, he or she becomes more and more repulsive to others, heterosexual and homosexual alike. The man becomes more effeminate, an "old queen," while the woman becomes a heartless, cruel, and "masculine" witch. The older gay and lesbian are depicted as both despised and rejected by younger homosexuals and as a threat to children who are the only accessible recipients of their perverse lust.

**53**

**New Script**     However, the script is being revised. Several surveys using both questionnaires and in-depth interviews of older gay men and lesbians have exposed the old drama. Most older gays and lesbians lead unremarkable lives and fare no worse (and sometimes better) than older heterosexuals. For example, in the first survey of older gay men, Kelly found that most were well adjusted, were not self-hating, had many friends, particularly in the gay community, had satisfactory sex lives with age-appropriate partners, and had some participation in activities of the local gay community.[3]

This author drew a similar profile of older gay men based on research in another area of the country. On measures such as self-acceptance, depression, and psychosomatic symptions, the great majority of older gays were well adjusted. Most had experienced a "lover" relationship and only a minority lived alone. Most had a network of friends and preferred friendships with age peers. In some ways older gays appeared better adjusted than younger gays. For instance, they were less likely to be anxious about their homosexuality and less likely to worry about concealment of their sexual identity.[4]

Although fewer older lesbians have been studied, research on this group has also debunked the old script. Older lesbians are not typically lonely and isolated. Although they may have fewer ties to their traditional families, well-established friendship networks and intimate love relationships provide support throughout the life span. Most have adjusted well. In at least one way the older lesbian is luckier than the older heterosexual woman. Whereas aging heterosexual women are routinely devalued by men as prospective intimate partners, loss of youth is less important as a standard of desirability in lesbian communities.[5]

Perhaps the most intriguing offshoot of this new examination of the realities of lesbian and gay aging is the discovery of ways in which being homosexual actually facilitates adaptation to aging. Two related phenomena identified by researchers may be dubbed "mastery of independence" and "mastery of stigma."[6] Both embody the idea that gays and lesbians, having had to master difficulties associated with their sexual preference early in life, are better able to cope with the stresses that accompany old age.

For example, most heterosexuals have family support systems (first, family of origin, and later, family of procreation) on which to rely for most of their lives. Then they grow old and lose their spouses and other members of their age cohort. This may be the first time they are forced to "make it on their own." Given the physical infirmities and social and economic constraints of old age, this is not a good time to learn new skills of independence. Gays and lesbians, on the other hand, cannot take support systems for granted in early life. Since their lifestyle makes it less likely that they will have traditional family supports after adolescence, they learn self-reliance and independence skills at an early age. These skills, in turn, make it easier to adapt to the losses of old age.

The "mastery of stigma" phenomenon also involves resolution of an early life crisis. According to this notion, adaptation to aging is impeded by the stigmatized status that accrues to older people in our culture. The older person must learn to deal with a society that belittles the personal abilities and devalues the individual importance of elders. Gays and lesbians will recognize the similarity of this process to the task of learning to cope with a stimatized identity, which gays and lesbians learn long before old age. As one older gay man noted, "If I learned how to handle being gay, I can certainly handle being old."

Yet another barrier on the road to a healthy, self-accepting old age is the loss of self-esteem that comes with the physical signs and diminished capacities of age. These changes represent a challenge to the woman's view of herself as "feminine" and to the man's view of himself as "masculine." To understand the trauma these changes can cause, one need only think of the older woman who loses interest in life as a result of menopause or the older man who is shamed by his inability to compete physically with younger men.

Certainly, these changes are difficult for most heterosexuals *and* homosexuals. However, gays and lesbians may have an advantage: Their self-concepts are not as dependent on traditional notions of what it means to be a man or a woman. For instance, a loss in physical strength for a gay man is less of a challenge to his self-esteem since he has already rejected society's view that a "good man" must be a "virile man." Similarly, the loss of a lesbian's youthful appearance is less of a challenge to her feelings of being a woman.

**Psychosocial Needs**

Despite these advantages, gay and lesbian aging has its pitfalls. The most remarkable finding of recent research is that older gays and lesbians are unremarkable: Their life patterns and psychosocial problems are more similar to, than different from, those of older persons in general.[7] The two most common concerns of both heterosexual and homosexual elderly are good health and good finances. Beyond this, there are some psychosocial needs that are unique to older gays and lesbians. These can be categorized into institutional problems, legal problems, and emotional needs.[8]

The most common institutional problems involve nursing homes and hospitals. An older gay or lesbian may be placed in a nursing home by relatives without consideration for the patient's lover or friends. Often the relatives have not been closely involved with the patient, but their decision-making power exceeds that of a lover of several decades. It is not uncommon, for instance, for a lover to be excluded from an intensive care unit of a hospital that will allow visits only from blood relatives. Most firms will not provide leave for an older gay or lesbian to care for a lover; perhaps more typically, the lover cannot even make such a request, for fear of reprisal. Once in the institution, if the older patient is labeled as gay or lesbian, poor treatment from staff and ostracism by other patients are common.[9]

When the legal system does not seek to punish gays and lesbians, it ignores them. This leaves many older gays and lesbians vulnerable. The most tragic example, and one which is common, is the case of the surviving partner. A surviving partner may lose a lifetime of investment and work to distant and often unsympathetic relatives, who have the legal, if not the moral, authority to claim the deceased's estate. This problem can be prevented by careful contractual agreements for gay and lesbian couples (see chapters by Kathleen Mayer and Fern Schwaber in this manual). But, unfortunately, the couple's desire to hide their relationship and the lack of sympathetic and informed legal help have combined to perpetuate such difficulties.

Older gays, like younger ones, are also subject to discrimination in employment and housing. While over forty municipalities offer some protection, most areas of the country do not.[10] And even in many areas where such protection is on the books, it is severely limited (e.g., applicable to public employment only) or requires lengthy legal action to be enforced.

The emotional needs of older gays and lesbians are not unique. Like all older people, they bend under the strain of life events: bereavement, physical illness, role losses. However, older gays and lesbians face the additional strain of coping with a homophobic world. Ironically, this homophobia is also characteristic of many agencies that are designed to help older people. This is exemplified by the social worker who refuses to understand why the client feels a total loss at the death of a "friend" and the agency that refuses to provide meeting space for a group of gay seniors. More sympathetic helping professionals may also be unable to help with emotional problems if they are unfamiliar with older gay and lesbian lifestyles, including such phenomena as ways of concealing a homosexual identity, community resources, and the role of friendship networks.

## How Social Workers Can Help

How can social workers be helpful to older lesbians and gays? A first step is to become informed about homosexuality and, in particular, to be familiar with the local gay and lesbian communities, which exist in almost every urban area. The worker must also confront his or her personal values and feelings about homosexuality and about sexuality in older adults. Social workers can also be active in organizing new services (such as discussion groups), participating in existing programs for older gays and lesbians (only a few exist presently), or working within mainstream social agencies to make services more responsive to older gays and lesbians.

Social workers can also tap the accumulated wisdom of gay and lesbian elders who have adapted successfully. This author did just that in his research. According to older gays and lesbians themselves, this is the formula for adapting well to old age:

1. Realize that being gay or lesbian makes no difference in how you react to growing older.

2. Keep active throughout your life.

3. Take care to maintain supportive friends.

4. Put some money away during your working years so you can live well in later years.

5. Associate with young and old, and keep up with new ideas.

6. Accept the limitations of physical aging. Don't try to turn the clock back.

7. Learn to get out of the spotlight. Realize that you are not the center of the universe.

8. Develop self-awareness: Accept yourself as a gay or lesbian person.

**Summary**  Inaccurate stereotypes about the horrors of old age for gays and lesbians have been refuted by a number of studies. In fact, in some ways gays and lesbians find it easier than heterosexuals to adapt to aging, and these differences may illuminate our understanding of the aging process in general. The life patterns and psychosocial needs of older gays and lesbians are remarkably similar to those of all elderly. Some concerns unique to older gays and lesbians involve institutional policies, the law, and finding informed and sympathetic help for emotional needs. Social workers must look to older gays and lesbians themselves to understand how to facilitate the aging process for this group.

**Notes**      1. For a discussion of how this estimate was derived, see Raymond M. Berger, "The Unseen Minority: Older Gays and Lesbians," *Social Work,* 27 (May 1982), p. 241, Note 1.

2. Alfred C. Kinsey, Wardell B. Pomeroy, and Clyde E. Martin, *Sexual Behavior in the Human Male;* and Kinsey et al., *Sexual Behavior in the Human Female* (Philadelphia: W. B. Saunders Co., 1948 and 1953, respectively).

3. Jim Kelly, "The Aging Male Homosexual: Myth and Reality," *Gerontologist,* 17 (August 1977), pp. 328–332.

4. Raymond M. Berger, *Gay and Gray: The Older Homosexual Man* (Urbana–Champaign: University of Illinois Press, 1982).

5. Sharon M. Raphael and Mina K. Robinson, "The Older Lesbian: Love Relationships and Friendship Patterns," *Alternative Lifestyles*, 3 (May 1980), pp. 207–229; Deborah Goleman Wolf, "Close Friendship Patterns of Older Lesbians," paper presented at the Annual Meeting of the Gerontological Society, Dallas, Tex., November 1978; and Wolf, "Life Cycle Changes of Older Lesbians and Gay Men," paper presented at the Annual Meeting of the Gerontological Society, San Diego, Calif., 1980.

6. J. Scott Francher and Janet Henkin, "The Menopausal Queen: Adjusting to Aging and the Male Homosexual," *American Journal of Orthopsychiatry*, 43 (July 1973), pp. 670–674; James J. Kelly and Myra T. Johnson, "Deviate Sex Behavior in the Aging: Social Definitions and the Lives of Older Gay People," in Oscar J. Kaplan, ed., *Psychopathology and Aging* (New York: Academic Press, 1979), pp. 243–258; and Douglas C. Kimmel, "Adjustment to Aging Among Gay Men," in Betty Berzon and Robert Leighton, eds., *Positively Gay* (Millbrae, Calif.: Celestial Arts Publishing Co., 1979), pp. 146–158.

7. Berger, *Gay and Gray;* and Wolf, "Life Cycle Changes of Older Lesbians and Gay Men."

8. Berger, "The Unseen Minority."

9. Raymond M. Berger, "Health Care for Lesbians and Gays: What Social Workers Should Know," *Journal of Social Work and Human Sexuality*, 1 (Spring 1983), pp. 59–73.

10. "Gay Rights Protections: United States and Canada" (New York: National Gay Task Force, September 1982).

# Gay Health Issues: Oppression Is a Health Hazard
## Caitlin Conor Ryan

**H**omophobia—the irrational fear of and hostility toward lesbian and gay people—remains in itself a major social disease rampant in our society with serious emotional and physical ramifications for those who succumb to it. Sadly, in our homophobic society both heterosexuals and homosexuals suffer from its contagions. In health care, homophobia causes needless physical and emotional anguish for lesbians and gay men, in addition to denying them accurate, unstigmatized, and humane diagnosis, treatment, and preventative health care. The lesbian and gay male populations remain, to the majority of health care providers, unacknowledged and unidentified, and so unseen. Our special problems, issues, and concerns usually remain untreated and unresearched by the dominant health care system. The oppression of gay bodies and spirits follows the oppression of gay lives.

In a society that does not validate lesbian/gay family structure, health care facilities and health insurance programs fail to recognize gay relationships. During medical emergencies (without a presigned medical power of attorney, which some gay couples are now initiating—see chapter by Fern W. Schwaber), lesbian and gay lovers/partners have *no power* to sign the legal consent forms that routinely afford heterosexual spouses legal guardianship for their partner's lives. Visiting privileges in intensive care units are restricted to what society and hospital staff consider to be the immediate biological or legal family, without concern for the emotional needs or wishes of the critically ill patient. Lesbian and gay patients, when so identified in emergency rooms and hospitals, are known to receive inferior, painful, and needlessly delayed medication and services. Lesbian and gay people presenting with a chemical dependency problem may find their sexual orientation the identified "disease" that physicians try to "cure," rather than focus on the alcoholism or drug addiction (see chapter by E. Sue Blume). The absence of health maintenance and outreach methods appropriate to the lesbian and gay community consistently denies our basic human right to health care services. The negligible response of the federal government to the AIDS public health crisis dating from 1981 further reflects an institutionalized denial of these basic human rights. Virginia Apuzzo, executive director of the National Gay Task Force, has verbalized the situation explicitly:

> There is no longer any debate regarding the link between the lethargy in the federal government's response to AIDS and the fact that so many of those stricken are gay men, and over forty per cent are people of color. Many of those are also gay. . . .The implications are shocking, unacceptable and unavoidable; that because they are gay or Haitian or IV drug users, these lives are thought to be expendable.[1]

**Exposure of Gay Identity**

In seeking treatment, many lesbians and gay men are reluctant to expose their identity to a potentially unsympathetic or hostile health care system or practitioner. Many will seek out lesbian or gay health services and health care workers. With recent national organizing and identification of lesbian and gay health facilities and practitioners, this becomes a more viable and preferable alternative, especially within the larger cities. Still, in more isolated or rural areas, and among those lesbians and gay men who have yet to recognize their supportive community, the fear of discovery, ridicule, and censure is still extreme and, sadly, warranted.

For the most part, physicians assume that their patients are heterosexual and will treat them accordingly. Lesbians presenting any variety of diverse complaints or problems will still be treated for reproductive concerns. Treatment time will focus on prescribing or expounding upon birth control techniques, cueing or coercing many lesbians to avoid a potentially unpleasant confrontation by denying their sexual selves. Important questions can remain unanswered or unasked. Since medical research lacks any significant or real data on lesbian health issues (for example, which infections may be transmitted between women and how or which health problems or concerns are prevalent within the lesbian community), practitioners will most often fail to address these areas in treatment. The burden for acquiring accurate data on lesbian and gay health care needs falls on lesbian and gay practitioners and researchers, since minority health concerns have not been a priority within health care delivery systems. Currently, the National Lesbian and Gay Health Foundation is conducting the first national survey of lesbian health care needs, which will greatly expand this area of concern for all providers and consumers.

That mothers can also be lesbians is more consistently ignored, although the stress of raising a child in a hostile environment is considerable. Other lesbians, seeking artificial or donor insemination, are often forced to conceal their sexual orientation even within alternative childbirth settings.

Gay men, too, are victimized by a health care delivery system that, misinformed and ignorant of gay health needs, often ignores or misdiagnoses their concerns. In a sexually repressed society, gay sex becomes particularly anxiety provoking so that many gay men are improperly screened and thus remain untreated for STDs (sexually transmitted disease). Amebiasis, for example, a sexually transmitted tropical amoeba, is often not included on the physician's list of differential diagnoses in a routine examination for abdominal complaints, so that a gay man with this disease can suffer needlessly and often for a long period of time before it is accurately diagnosed and treated. Following a routine operation, such as for hemorrhoids, a physician who assumes the heterosexuality of his or her patient will fail to discuss the resumption of anal intercourse, a subject the patient will often be too embarrassed to raise. Many physicians, recoiling at the possibility of same-sex lovemaking, yet sensing or learning that a patient is gay, will purposely avoid the subject or will give inaccurate information. Often excessively painful examinations or treatment will follow revelation of a gay sexual orientation.

**AIDS** A frightening component of the recent AIDS crisis is the hysteria among health care workers and public servants in their treatment of gay men and other people who have AIDS. Social workers and nurses in hospitals have refused to work with people with AIDS, enter their rooms, take histories, or perform routine personal care. Ambulance drivers have refused to transport people with AIDS, and firemen and policemen have demanded special masks and gloves for handling gay men who may or may not have AIDS. Although current theories seem to indicate that AIDS is transmitted through intimate sexual contact or blood products and that no health care workers (not in high-risk groups) who have treated people with AIDS according to prescribed guidelines have contracted the disease, panic and homophobia are increasing exponentially with the spread of AIDS.

### Incidence

At the writing of this article, as information changes daily, a total of 6,857 cases of AIDS have been reported in the United States and Puerto Rico.[2] Three-fourths of these cases are among sexually active gay men between the ages of 20 and 49. The fatality rate of AIDS is extremely high— approximately 75 percent within three to four years after the initial diagnosis is made. AIDS (Acquired Immune Deficiency Syndrome) is the first-known, naturally occurring breakdown of the body's immune system (see chapter by Paul Paroski). All individuals who have AIDS are immune suppressed; however, the reverse is not always true.

### Costs

There is no single course to the disease. There is also no doubt that AIDS is spreading rapidly, with the number of cases doubling every six months. The cost of the disease is astounding. Estimates by Dr. Jeanne Kassler in May 1982 show that hospital costs alone for the first 300 cases were $18 million.[3] An average hospital stay for a person with AIDS is $100,000. People who have AIDS quickly exhaust their financial resources, especially since the debilitating nature of the disease often forces them to stop working. Many are fired when their employers learn that they have AIDS, or co-workers conspire against them for fear of contracting it themselves. People with AIDS are frequently evicted by landlords and roommates; relationships between lovers and friends can become strained or drift off. Many describe feeling like lepers or pariahs. Yet the strength and dignity of our brothers and sisters who speak of "fighting for their lives" are profoundly moving and reenforce the resolve of those of us who work with them.

Part of the fight is provision of direct services and part is in moving resistant federal and state bureaucracies to appropriate adequate funds for research. This is a long and costly process, because it takes approximately ten years to test and prepare a medical treatment for marketing once it has been discovered. Advocacy is essential, as is an understanding of some of the unique concerns relevant to gay people who have AIDS.

### Personal Issues

Generally speaking, gay men place great emphasis on body image, physical looks, and health. Sexuality is an important aspect of their lives and an expression of freedom. A disease that negatively affects all of these areas by ravaging their bodies and denying them sexual expression in familiar ways is seen as drastically limiting their life patterns.

Dependency issues for men who have been successful by societal standards (the mean income for gay men with AIDS is $26–27,000 annually, and the median years of education is 16), become paramount.[4] Many men for the first time find their sexuality open to question by parents, business associates, and old family friends who may not have known that they were gay. Ordinarily, coming out represents a lifelong process of self-actualization, discovery, and growth. It takes time, courage, and self-confidence to come out. It also takes time for other family members to work through their own issues and negative stereotypes about homosexuality. Being forced to acknowledge one's gay identity when a disease like AIDS is diagnosed can present an additional burden and shock for the patient and family. Sensitivity of the worker to the spiritual needs of their gay clients, which may just be surfacing as a result of the poor prognosis of their disease, as well as the worker's awareness of the availability of gay ministries and religious resources, can provide clients with an important outlet to work through anger and fear about their disease.

## Gay Community Response

Gay community response to the AIDS crisis has been positive in providing much-needed services, financial assistance, lobbying efforts, and media attention. Local AIDS organizations have recently grouped themselves into an international Federation of AIDS Related Organizations to share information and resources and support a national lobbying effort to acquire funding for AIDS research. Guidelines for meeting the needs of people with AIDS, who are not "victims" and who are only "patients" some of the time, were released along with national policy statements on infection control, blood banks, and public education at the second National AIDS Forum.[5] Copies of these reports and additional information on AIDS can be obtained from your local AIDS organization.

## Related Conditions

Medical personnel state that what we are currently seeing with the AIDS epidemic is only the "tip of the iceberg," because the gestation period is unclear (although it is estimated to be from a few months to four years) and the mobility of the population at risk is significant. Terms such as "pre-AIDS" or "prodromal AIDS" have been used interchangeably (and with the current level of knowledge, inaccurately), for a cluster of vague and disquieting symptoms, such as chronic swollen lymph nodes, wasting syndrome, and night sweats. Recently termed ARC or AIDS Related Complex, these symptoms have evolved into full blown AIDS—an immune deficiency with the presence of Kaposi's sarcoma or an opportunistic infection—in some 15 percent of the cases studied. Individuals diagnosed with ARC can live in a twilight of uncertainty in terms of what this condition may mean or what it can become.

Because the current Centers for Disease Control surveillance definition of AIDS (given above) has been adopted as the official AIDS criteria in order to qualify for social security benefits, individuals who are disabled with ARC, and in some instances severely, cannot receive these benefits. Many workers are involved with pressuring federal and state agencies to redefine their guidelines for AIDS. In many communities, public education on prevention, focused on limiting sexual contacts, redefining relationships, and encouraging safe sex behaviors with alternative social outlets, is developing. Support for workers is also essential, and many AIDS related groups provide support for counselors and group leaders.

**Gay Health Organizations**   The national lesbian/gay health movement has increasingly provided a base of support for lesbian/gay workers, as well as students in professional schools, who along with their clients suffer from the stress of potential ridicule, hostility, or possible job loss from self-disclosure. The National Lesbian and Gay Health Foundation, an outgrowth of the National Gay Health Coalition (comprised of the lesbian, gay, and bisexual caucuses of the major professional health-related organizations, as well as other specialized national lesbian and gay health organizations) yearly sponsors a national lesbian/gay health conference in a major U.S. city. Here, lesbian and gay health workers from all over the country can gather to share information, increase support, and expand advocacy procedures within their professional organization. For example, both the National Committee on Lesbian and Gay Issues of NASW and the Commission on Gay/Lesbian Issues of the Council on Social Work Education are members of the National Gay Health Coalition. As such, they combine with other professional gay health organizations to affect the national health care delivery system. In the professional schools, they struggle to implement change by introducing and teaching appropriate, informed courses on lesbian and gay lifestyles, issues, and concerns.

Nongay practitioners who wish to serve their lesbian and gay clients or patients humanely and adequately must be willing to examine their biases, to discard their presumptions of innate heterosexuality, to raise their consciousness, and to increase their sensitivity to the societal oppression of lesbian and gay people.

**Suggestions for Intervention**
- Avoid assuming that everyone is heterosexual.
- Avoid using language that is biased, sexist, or judgmental. If office applications or information forms are written in a way that is clearly heterosexist, change them.

For example, *marriage* can be changed to read *primary relationship;* *husband* or *wife* can be phrased as *significant other, partner, lover;* and so on.

- Familiarize yourself with periodicals on lesbian and gay health care, oppression, and lifestyles. Have these as available for patients in waiting rooms or in consultation as any other medically related materials.

- Contact the lesbian and gay caucuses within your professional organization for information on consciousness-raising groups or training sessions for nongay practitioners working with lesbian and gay clients. If you are a lesbian or gay male, join the caucus. Oppression is maintained by isolating and silencing us.

- Attend the workshops on lesbian and gay issues at your annual professional conferences or at other related conferences.

- Become aware of the resources available in your community for lesbians and gay men so that you can refer your clients or patients to support systems and relevant services.

1. Virginia Apuzzo, Address to the Plenary Session, **Notes** Fifth National Lesbian/Gay Health Conference (following the Second National AIDS Forum), Denver, Colo., June 1983.

2. "Weekly AIDS Update," Centers for Disease Control, Atlanta, Ga., 12 November 1984.

3. Jeanne Kassler, *Gay Men's Health: A Guide to the AID Syndrome and Other Sexually Transmitted Diseases* (New York: Harper & Row, 1983).

4. Information given by James Curran, MD, MPH, Southeastern Conference for Lesbians and Gay Men, Atlanta, Ga., April 1983.

5. National Association of People with AIDS (NAPWA), "Guidelines for Meeting the Needs of People with AIDS," Fifth National Lesbian/Gay Health Conference (following National AIDS Forum), Denver, Colo., June 1983.

# Sexually Transmitted Diseases
## Paul A. Paroski, Jr.

Anyone who is sexually active runs the risk of contracting any of the many diseases known to be transmitted sexually. Although this problem is not exclusive to one subgroup of the population, the incidence is extremely high in the gay male population and extremely low in the lesbian population. Regardless of the individual's sexual practices and preferences, we must be aware of the reality of these diseases. There are several basic principles common to all of the sexually transmitted diseases:[1]

1. The greater the number of different sexual partners, the greater the risk is of acquiring a sexually transmitted disease.

2. Statistics demonstrate that anonymous sexual contacts create a greater risk of contracting one of these diseases than do known sexual contacts.

3. Certain types of sexual activity result in a higher risk of transmitting disease than do other types of activities.

4. All sexually active individuals should be routinely screened for the common sexually transmitted diseases. Many times, the symptoms of these diseases may not be apparent, and therefore, the condition may go untreated.

### Gonorrhea

**Common Diseases** Gonorrhea (often called "the clap," the "drip") may only be transmitted via sexual contact with an infected partner. Initially, it is a localized disease, primarily affecting the throat, the rectum, the urethra in the male, or the cervix in the female. The location of the disease depends on direct sexual contact of the area. If left untreated, it may cause scarring of the urethra in the male or spread to the fallopian tubes in the female and cause scarring. Furthermore, it can have systemic spread causing fever, arthritis, heart disease, meningitis, and other diseases. These complications can be prevented by early detection and treatment. The symptoms usually appear two to ten days after sexual contact. They are as follows:

Penis—a discharge of pus and/or pain upon urination; or in a small number of individuals, no symptoms.

*Cervix*—usually without symptoms; however, a whitish discharge from the vagina may be noted, and some pain on urination.

*Throat*—usually without symptoms; in rare cases, a sore throat.

*Rectum*—usually without symptoms; however, a significant number of individuals note pussy discharge, a feeling of fullness, excessive gas, or pain on defecation.

## Syphilis

Syphilis can only be contracted from contact with an infected person. Because it is a systemic disease, it is dangerous in that it may cause damage to many parts of the body. The symptoms are easily overlooked. They are described as follows:

*Primary Stage*—occurs ten to ninety days after exposure to an infected person. Initially, a painless sore, called a chancre, develops at the site of infection. This can be on the penis, in the vagina, in the mouth, in the rectum, or at other locations. It eventually disappears without treatment.

*Secondary Stage*—may develop anywhere from two weeks to six months after the appearance of the chancre. The symptoms include a skin rash anywhere on the body; loss of hair; fever; fatigue; swollen lymph glands; sores around the mouth, genitals, and/or arms. These symptoms disappear without treatment.

*Late Stage* (or untreated syphilis)—can occur several years after symptoms of the secondary stage disappear. Late-stage syphilis produces severe complications of the heart, blood vessels, nervous system, and other organ systems.

### Nongonococcal Urethritis (NGU)

Nongonococcal urethritis, sometimes called nonspecific urethritis, is an inflammation of the urethra in the male that is not caused by gonorrhea. It is thought to be caused by an organism called chlamydia. It is usually acquired through sexual contact. The symptoms include burning upon urination, slight urethral discharge, and/or tenderness in the tip of the penis. Treatment is usually required.

### Genital Herpes

Genital herpes is a disease caused by a virus (herpes virus) and is usually contracted by sexual contact. After an unknown period of time following sexual contact, small painful blisters develop in the genital area, usually on the penis, in the vagina, or around the rectum. These may be severely painful; however, they begin to resolve within four to five days. They may be associated with systemic symptoms such as fever and lethargy. There is no known cure for this disease, and reinfections or recurrent disease is common.

### Venereal Warts

Venereal warts are caused by a virus and may be transmitted by sexual contact. These can develop from one to six months after contact with an infected person. They appear as soft pink or red warts on the penis, in the vagina, and/or around or within the rectum. They may increase in size and become painful or bleed. They are treated by chemical or electrical destruction (electrodessication) or in some cases by surgery.

### Hepatitis

Viral hepatitis, type A, type B, non-A, or non-B, can be spread by sexual contact. There is an extremely high incidence of type B, as well as type A, hepatitis in the gay male population. It is caused by a virus, and its early symptoms include fatigue, loss of appetite, nausea, vomiting, aversion to smoke and alcohol, low-grade fever, and muscle pains. These symptoms are then followed by jaundice (yellowing of the skin and dark urine), abdominal pain, and extreme lethargy. The range of severity of viral hepatitis varies from extremely mild, when the individual may not notice the illness, to severe, when hospitalization is required. No specific medications are routinely used in hepatitis. One provides symptomatic care, to help the person through the disease, and to allow the body's normal systems to eradicate the disease. Hepatitis B can be prevented by means of a vaccine, and all sexually active gay men should receive this immunization.

### Parasitic Diseases

There is a whole group of parasitic diseases that may be contracted by sexual contact. The most common of these are amebiasis and giardiasis. They are caused by amebas or giardia respectively. These organisms are spread through fecal-oral contamination, therefore, any sexual activity involving the rectum may spread these diseases. The symptoms include abdominal pain, nausea, diarrhea, change in bowel habits, and/or generalized lethargy. There are various drugs that can treat these diseases.

### Enteric Infections (Bacterial)

There are several bacterial enteric infections that can be contracted via sexual contact. The best known include shigella and salmonella. These are spread by fecal-oral contamination. As with the parasites, any sexual activity involving the rectum can spread these diseases. The symptoms include severe cramps, diarrhea, usually a high fever, and generalized muscle pain. These diseases may last several days, and specific therapy may be indicated.

### Infestations

Of the several types of infestations, the most common are crabs (pediculosis) and scabies. These are spread by close contact with an infected person. Contact need not be sexual, and these infestations can be transmitted by sharing the same bed, clothes, or towel. The mites live on the infested person's body, causing irritation, sores, and itching. There are several drugs that will destroy the organisms.

### Acquired Immune Deficiency Syndrome (AIDS)

AIDS is a disease that seems to be transmitted sexually or via intimate contact. There is *no* evidence that it can be spread by simple social contact. The disease is manifested by a breakdown of a person's immune system and the development of unusual infections, including pneumocystis carinii pneumonia (PCP) of Kaposi's sarcoma. There are several symptoms that may be consistent with AIDS. These include swollen lymph glands for more than two months in duration; unexpected weight loss of ten pounds or more in less than two months; an unexplained fever for more than one week; periods of waking up drenched or sweaty over several weeks; unexplained diarrhea; a pink to purple flat or raised lesion that has recently occurred and does not resolve; persistent dry hacking cough not due to a cold; or the feeling of being unable to catch one's breath. Should an individual notice any of these symptoms, he or she should be referred to a physician.

**Conclusion**  As one can see, there are numerous medical conditions associated with sexual contact or close contact with other individuals. A knowledge of these common problems is important in dealing with any sexually active individual. However, these conditions are more prevalent in the gay male population and are often overlooked. It is the duty of the health care provider to be on the lookout for these conditions, in providing holistic care to an individual.

**Note**       1. The National Coalition of Gay Sexually Transmitted Disease Services published in 1984 a pamphlet titled *Guidelines and Recommendations for Healthful Gay Sexual Activity,* which may be helpful to the client who is unaware of the need for caution and hygienic practices as part of responsible sexual behavior. This pamphlet may be ordered from NCGSTDS, P.O. Box 239, Milwaukee, Wis. 53201.

# Psychosocial Issues Related to the Diagnosis of AIDS
## Gary G. Treese

Within the past few years, a new disease, Acquired Immune Deficiency Syndrome (AIDS), has been recognized. There are considerable psychosocial implications with the diagnosis of this syndrome, and social workers and other helping professionals should be aware of the special considerations that these patients bring into the social work setting.

First, a brief discussion of the syndrome and the at-risk population is in order. This syndrome was first noted in male homosexuals and drug abusers, but it has now been seen in Haitian refugees, patients with hemophilia, and the female sexual partner of a heterosexual drug abuser. The most basic abnormality of AIDS appears to be a profound depression in cellular immunity. The disease was originally recognized at the Centers for Disease Control in 1980 when clusters of cases of pneumocystis carinii pneumonia suddenly began appearing in otherwise healthy adults who were either male homosexuals or drug abusers. These patients were frequently infected with other opportunistic agents—infectious organisms that only infect humans with compromised immune systems or that are more severely damaging to such individuals (for example, toxoplasma, candidiasis, cryptosporidiasis, cytomegalovirus, and severe herpes simplex). In addition, some of these patients were developing Kaposi's sarcoma, which had been extremely rare in the United States.

As of December 19, 1983, 3,000 AIDS patients had been reported to the Centers for Disease Control. A total of 1,283 (43 percent) of reported patients were known to have died.

**The Disease**

This chapter was originally given as part of a panel presentation at the Department of Psychiatry, Baylor College of Medicine, Houston, Tex., November 2, 1983.

73

Of the 3,000 patients, 90 percent were between 20 and 49 years old. Fifty-nine percent of the cases occurred among white males, 26 percent among blacks, and 14 percent among persons of Hispanic origin. Women accounted for 7 percent of the cases. Large metropolitan areas continue to report the highest number of cases. Groups at highest risk of acquiring AIDS continue to be homosexual and bisexual men (71 percent of cases) and intravenous drug abusers (17 percent); 12 percent of patients have other or unknown risk factors.[1]

**Issues and Ramifications** This chapter addresses some of the critical issues that confront the gay male with AIDS, his family, and caregivers. The ideas are based on my personal experience working in Houston with gay males with AIDS over the last two years. Some of the psychosocial ramifications of this serious health problem in relation to the gay male population are also discussed. The AIDS phenomenon has forced many previously healthy young men to view themselves as persons in a life-threatening or at best life-altering situation, and the person with AIDS presents himself to the mental health practitioner just as any person seeking help dealing with such a situation. The seriousness of AIDS has caused another large segment of the gay population to be called the "worried well." With the significant media coverage of AIDS and the growing number of persons actually diagnosed, the numbers of "worried well" are growing also.

A number of issues come to the forefront of therapeutic intervention when one is treating a person with a life-threatening illness. The focus in this chapter is on life-cycle issues and loss. Loss is viewed in terms of loss of control, loss of the sense of identity, and finally loss of relationships.[2] It is to be remembered that, just as the physical manifestations of AIDS are variable, so too are the psychological responses of the affected individuals.

### Denial and Anger

Most people diagnosed with AIDS are in the prime of life, so the typical response is one of denial and anger. For the gay person, the defense mechanism of denial is a well-developed and often-used defense. Gay people have spent many years practicing denial of their sexual orientation, at some expense to their identity. So, to be diagnosed as having a life-threatening illness brings up the usual reaction of denial (followed by anger). This denial may be protracted and deeper.

For a gay person, anger is another response that may have been suppressed and poorly directed, so the anger may be more intense and more self-directed. When one considers that the sexual transmission theory of AIDS is so prevalent, one can easily understand that the person with AIDS feels that his much-fought-for sexual identity is now going to be the literal death of him.

### Loss

Eventually, especially with therapeutic assistance, the three-faceted issue of loss must be directly confronted—specifically, loss of control, loss of the sense of identity, and loss of relationships. When a person is diagnosed as having AIDS, his sense of control dissolves in coming face-to-face with the limits of time. He experiences loss of control in many areas—over his body, over disease and pain, over emotional boundaries, and ultimately over life itself.

*Control.* For the AIDS patient, the loss of control in all these areas is potentiated by the newness and lack of factual medical knowledge of AIDS. This complicates even more the work of the physical and psychosocial caregivers.

For the person with AIDS, the unknown lies ahead like an uncharted territory, without landmarks or guides. Learning to live with AIDS involves a constant adaptation to tolerating risks and the unknown. This, however, is where the gay person has an advantage: The gay person's very existence has long been filled with risk and uncertainty. His adaptational skills are usually well developed—if not overly developed—in his struggle to maintain control over these risks and uncertainties.

*Identity.* Loss of the sense of identity is the second significant process for the person with a life-threatening illness. An individual's identity may broaden to incorporate new facets, but its essential configuration remains constant over time. What, then, are the implications of a life-threatening illness for one's sense of identity?

Initially, the disease is viewed as an external intruder. The patient refers to "the illness, the cancer" as if to assert, "This illness is separate from me." Over time the patient begins to speak more easily of "my illness, my cancer." These subtle shifts in language are testimony to a significant process: What began as an external entity has been transformed into an internalized part of one's physical and emotional self-concept. The task is to create a balance whereby an individual's identity as a patient is incorporated into the broader spectrum of his identity in general without overshadowing it.

Attaining a solid sense of identity is another crucial process that many gay people have been struggling with in an environment that often regards their sexual orientation as alien. The person with a life-threatening illness fights not to be identified totally with his disease. The pervasive fear is of being defined exclusively in terms of being a patient, both by oneself and by others.

The same issue applies to being a homosexual person. So often the search for identity is so intense that gay people go through a period of narrowing their view of their identity to their gayness alone. Some people never leave that stage. This constriction of identity—combined with having AIDS, the "gay disease"—can be a particularly damaging constellation for the psychological well-being of some people, who tend to experience their identity as pervasively undermined.

*Relationships.* Finally, the loss of relationships is a key factor that persons with AIDS must deal with. Although issues of control and identity belong primarily to the patient, the loss of relationships is shared by the patient, the family, and the caregiver. All are grappling with the inevitable transformation of presence into absence. Absence—physical, psychological, and social—connotes profound and total emptiness. Absence is a part of every loss, but an undercurrent of isolation and abandonment is not. However, for the person with AIDS, isolation is literal and abandonment may have already occurred because of the individual's homosexual orientation. AIDS patients must deal not only with the loss of relationships because they may die, they must deal with the loss of relationships because they have been diagnosed as having AIDS, an illness for which there is no known cause or cure and the possible contagiousness of which may frighten away significant others.

Another serious strain on relationships for the gay person related to this diagnosis is that they are forced into revealing their homosexual orientation to family, friends, employers, and health care workers, all of whom may be more or less homophobic. The issue of sexual orientation is of central concern for many people with AIDS. They have been struggling with or have won the battle for sexual identity, only to be told that they have now acquired a disease that is seemingly associated with that very struggle.

## The 'Worried Well'

In addition to those persons who have been diagnosed as having AIDS, there is a much larger group of people who are anticipating the diagnosis or worrying about the possibility. The implications for mass anxiety and depression are important considerations. Some of the same issues confront both the "worried well" and persons with AIDS, especially the issue of the sense of identity.

Many gay people are caught in the struggle for a sense of identity. Many are seeing the AIDS epidemic as proof that they are sinful and unclean. Jerry Falwell and Billy Graham have even implicated God in this mysterious health problem. Some individuals are seeking therapeutic intervention with their chief complaint being anxiety over AIDS. They report symptoms of sleep disturbance, loss of sexual interest, a preoccupation with symptoms, and a general malaise. They, too, are experiencing their psychological and physical well-being as being undermined and are struggling to regain a firm foundation.

The reaction to this problem by many gay people has been one of mobilization and action, a response that points out the remarkable adaptive skills of this group and speaks to the innate call to action in the face of fear. The AIDS epidemic is causing some real changes in the gay male population of this country.

Like herpes, AIDS is causing many people to look again at their sexual activity. Merle Hoffman, a family planning counselor in New York, makes an interesting analogy:

Women are confronted with this sexual truth: the price that all women may pay for their sexual activities in terms of pregnancy, abortion, child birth, fear and anxiety for a sex act that men can and often do walk away from unconcerned.[3]

AIDS has changed all that. For the first time since penicillin eliminated the fear of venereal disease, men—particularly gay men—are now questioning whether sex should be more discriminant. Anonymous, casual intercourse can actually have consequences and these consequences can be life threatening. Now, for the first time, men may have to "pay a price" for a sexual interlude—something that women have always had to deal with.

The ritual of women checking for signs of a hoped for menstruation can be equated with men now checking for sores, swollen glands, or blotches on the skin. Pregnancy under these circumstances and AIDS are both unwanted and unplanned-for consequences of a moment of sexual pleasure.

I do not think that many gay men recognize this analogy; however, some are in touch with the reality that one sex act can have serious implications to their health. They are now being forced to contemplate the consequences of sexual activity. For those whose sense of identity is narrowly focused on sexual activity, this is proving to be devastating. Many continue to practice their well-developed defense of denial, but others have realized that communication, intimacy, and love are far more important than casual sexual encounters. It is certainly hoped that this realization will facilitate the containment of the spread of this tragic disease.

**Notes**

1. Centers for Disease Control, "Update: AIDS in the U.S.," *Morbidity and Mortality Weekly Report*, Vol. 32, No. 52 (Atlanta, Ga.: Public Health Service, U.S. Department of Health & Human Services, January 6, 1984), pp. 688–689.

2. Barbara M. Sourkes, *The Deepening Shade* (Pittsburgh, Pa.: University of Pittsburgh Press, 1982).

3. Merle Hoffman (Executive Director, Choices: The Creative Health Organization), Letter to the Editor, *Womanews* (New York City), October 1983.

# Substance Abuse
# (Of Being Queer, Magic Pills, and Social Lubricants)
## E. Sue Blume

**H**eroin. Alcohol. Caffeine. Marijuana. Tranquilizers. Stimulants. Sleeping pills. The consequences of the abuse of these and other mood-altering substances are staggering. What Americans seek as temporary "solutions" to the stresses of their daily existence often *become* the problem, leading to serious emotional, physical, and spiritual consequences, destroyed relationships, even death. There is no magic pill to make the pains of daily life go away. And what of those for whom the pains of daily life are only the beginning, who must deal constantly with the practical and emotional consequences of being fags, fairies, queers, dykes, lezzies, illegal, immoral, sick? In common with other oppressed groups, lesbians and gays are susceptible to the seductiveness of chemicals that take away that pain. Often, they are then further victimized by the very agencies to which they turn for help.

**A Population at Particular Risk**

It is not that homosexuality is a sickness that easily leads to other sicknesses, as many traditional theoreticians would have us believe. Rather, it is the position of lesbians and gay men in society that results in their special vulnerability to drug and alcohol abuse. This traditional view can be called "blaming the victim" and can itself be seen as one of the consequences of homophobia.

### The Gay Bar

In America, alcohol and certain other drugs are inexorably tied to the seeking of and participation in sex, romance, and love. For lesbians/gays, this situation is exacerbated by the fact that they must concentrate interpersonal activities into certain times and places. The gay bar has historically been the protected place where homosexual persons could meet, socialize, be the dominant culture, make sexual contacts, start relationships, hold hands, dance, belong—all the things that nongays can integrate into the totality of their lives and therefore take for granted. While today there are alternatives to the bar scene within the homosexual community, it remains an integral part of gay male culture, and continues to be important—though much less so—to lesbians as well. Such prolonged exposure to the culture of alcohol puts a substantial portion of the homosexual community in particular jeopardy for overuse and alcoholism.

### The 'God, Was I Drunk Last Night' Syndrome: The 'Secret' and 'Coming Out'

Being drunk can allow an individual who wishes to maintain the label "heterosexual" to disavow responsibility for homosexual acts. The first time, you can probably believe it. The second time, you might have your doubts. The third time, you can assume the person is either lesbian/gay—or alcoholic—or maybe both. This can also apply to the use of other drugs, of course. Use of alcohol and other chemicals can become abuse as the individual relies on such substances in order to maintain denial of a lesbian/gay orientation or to cope with the fears and guilt accompanying initial self-identity. For those who accept their lesbian/gay identities, the process of coming out to others or the daily pressures and problems created by an oppressive, homophobic society not counterbalanced by rewarding support systems may prove to be too overwhelming. In such instances, substance use/abuse is perceived as a welcome armor in a hostile world.

### Denial

In addition to certain behaviors, there are feelings and an identity that lesbians, gay men, and bisexual individuals—many of whom are not yet self-labeled as such—need to dismiss, to deny. The awareness of these feelings and their meanings can best be deadened through the use of chemicals. However, at the first moment of clarity, the horrible question What if I'm ———? manifests itself once again. More and more frequently, it is pushed away with drugs and/or booze. And so *use* becomes *abuse*.

Denial is also a fundamental characteristic of substance abuse per se. It is the process that allows the abuser not to perceive, and therefore not to integrate to take responsibility for those problems that develop as the abuse gets out of hand. The abuser simply does not see the drug or alcohol use as the problem. It is, in fact, seen as a *solution* to terrible life stresses. Chemical abuse further feeds the denial that is made necessary in order to allow continuation of addiction. It is a cycle that is finally broken as the abuser affirms, Yes, I am an alcoholic or addicted person. This first of the "12 Steps" used by Alcoholics Anonymous is similar to the breaking of denial about homosexuality and is a first step in coming out in a homophobic world. However, the subsequent stages of leaving a secret, isolated, interpersonally stressful existence and moving into the "real world" consequences of living an openly gay lifestyle provide stressors that some can only bear with the "help" of substances that deaden the experience. Clearly, the developmental stages of the maturing gay identity can only be worked through if one's head is clear enough to experience both the crises *and* the victories that accompany growth.

**Lesbian Substance Abusers**

As with other areas of socialization, information about male alcoholics has been assumed to apply to female alcoholics as well. So too, the lesbian alcoholic or drug abuser is the most invisible and the most misunderstood, contending with being homosexual, female, and substance abusing. She has special problems, beyond the fact that she is expected to conform to sexist treatment facilities. In addition, the antecedents and manifestations of her alcoholism differ significantly from those of male alcoholics. If married, she is often trapped both by financial dependence and responsibility as primary caretaker of the children. She, like her heterosexual sister, may therefore seek other escapes—closet drinking or tranquilizers. The single lesbian must still deal with an upbringing that teaches her to be half a person, a society that rarely encourages her to develop her own power, and a "gay community" that sometimes makes little room for her as a woman, and that is, in fact, as male dominated as the straight world from which she seeks refuge. If the lesbian seeks help, those few treatment centers that are designed to meet the needs of "gays" often exclude her by their failure to recognize the special needs and identity of women; the storefront that is the "last resort" for gay men is as useless to her as heterosexually dominated centers are for many gay men.

**Treatment, Abuse, and Neglect** Many estimates on alcoholism among gays and lesbians project a rate that is considerably higher than that of the general population; the most commonly cited of these is the Fifield study.[1] Due to the invisibility of most lesbians and gay men (whose identity is frequently hidden even from themselves, at which time they are at tremendous risk for chemical abuse), the actual rate is, of course, impossible to calculate. What is known, however, is that most agencies report only a handful of homosexual clients at most. This means that drug- and alcohol-abusing lesbians and gay men are either not seeking treatment—and are dying—or that they are not being honest with their therapists—and still are dying. For we must remember that we are talking about a problem that is ultimately fatal. Even among those agencies that recognize the special needs of lesbian and gay clients, efforts are rarely made to accommodate them in any way.

That drug and alcohol treatment facilities replicate the prejudice and ignorance found in other therapeutic settings is reflected in the often-asked question, Which do I cure first, the alcoholism or the homsexuality? Agency policy discriminates in a number of ways; the attitudes of professionals in substance abuse reflect those of social workers, psychologists, and psychiatrists. In addition, there are issues that are particularly characteristic of drug and alcohol treatment.

### Paraprofessionals and Peers

Treatment of chemical abuse relies heavily on the services of paraprofessionals who are either recovering themselves or who come from chemically dependent families. They work as counselors and offer supportive services through self-help groups, where part of the recovery process is to help other recovering people. These individuals sometimes hold very traditional values, values that have not been challenged through professional training or supervision. Out of the need of women and sexual minorities to find nonjudgmental peer support, groups such as Gay and/or Lesbian AA, Gay Al-Anon, and Alcoholics Together have arisen to provide alternatives to existing groups and values. Women-only alcoholism halfway houses are a fortunate recent development and are recommended for lesbian alcoholics.

In the field of drug abuse, the therapeutic community (TC), was originated by male addicts whose values reflect the streets from which they came. They are often decidedly sexist, placing value on rigid sex-role behavior based on male rules.[2] While many centers are working to change this prejudice, many continue to manifest a reluctance to evaluate new ideas about women, men, sexuality, and sex-role behavior. A few agencies have been developed to serve lesbian, gay, or women clients exclusively, but the solution really lies in changing existing agencies so that everyone can be served.

For those lesbian or gay clients who become involved with substance- and alcohol-abuse treatment, several issues particularly manifest themselves. These are as follows: **Treatment Issues**

### Con Artists

Chemical abusers become expert manipulators in defense of their abusing careers. They use every possible defense to protect the habit. When a lesbian or gay client works with an undereducated nongay worker, the client may effectively use her or his sexual orientation to put the worker on the defensive, for instance, by saying, You don't understand—which may indeed be quite accurate.

### Significant Others

Abuse of alcohol or drugs creates a family in crisis. It is crucial that all significant others be involved in the recovery process, including, for example, the family of origin or same-sex lover. Many therapists do not know how to handle a client whose homophobic parents have abandoned her or him. They may not consider including a lover or partner in problem solving. The agency must understand the role that the gay or lesbian community plays in providing an extended family for homosexual individuals.

### Self-Esteem and Identity

The average abusing client must conquer severely low self-esteem and work hard to develop a new, drug-free identity. Identity formation and low self-image are fulcrum issues for lesbians and gay men as well. Agencies and workers must understand this problem and know what resources are available for its solution.

*Stigma,* so much a part of the issue of chemical abuse, is another aspect of the life of the lesbian and gay man. In order for treatment to address all these issues adequately, workers must have comprehensive, current, nonbiased information available, both for their own skill enhancement and to provide clients with information and support in using community resources, literature, the lesbian/gay culture, and the gifts—yes, the *gifts*—of being a gay man or lesbian.

*Sexuality* is a major concern for both the client and worker. The client must deal with past sexual activities and learn new social rules. The worker must be comfortable discussing intimate (homo)sexual details, although she or he may be none too comfortable discussing sexuality—at all!

In recovery, clients must be doubly strong in order to cope with the stigma and aftershocks of being chemically dependent and with the stresses of being different in an oppressive world. This requires tremendous inner strength and an ability to reach out for support from resources other than drugs and alcohol. Such resources include networks of gay/lesbian groups as well as recovery peer groups. The client, therefore, must not only meet the challenge of individual survival, but must find new ways to influence the ignorance and hostility of the world to which she or he must return.

### Training

**Resources and Solutions**

Staff training—including attention to both information and attitudes—is a necessary first step toward better meeting the needs of lesbian and gay clients. But it is only the first step. Chronic chemical dependence is a holistic problem, requiring psychological, social, physical, vocational, legal, and environmental attention. Whether abusing alcohol, street drugs, or prescription medication, the individual abandons the real world, reducing social contacts to persons who are themselves involved with drugs or alcohol; the selected substance(s) of abuse become the person's emotional, social, problem-solving, and entertainment outlet. In all of these areas, the service providers must recognize and address the special needs of lesbian and gay clients. For example, this includes permitting visits from lovers in a detoxification hospital if the policy is "family" only. The vocational counselor who believes in employment stereotypes and is working toward developing job alternatives for the lesbian/gay client must consider the real meaning of "job alternatives." Following this, the recovering person should have a new, positive community to reenter—a community that enhances both the person's sobriety and the sexual/affectional lifestyle— a community that does not center on gay bars. Lesbian/gay peer recovery groups should be located or created.

### Treating the System

The service system must change at all levels. Funding, ever political and frequently religious, must be available to meet training, program, and special service needs. (What chance does a grant for *lesbians/gays* have?) Administrators must translate affirmation of homosexuality into policy, encouraging training and programs, hiring openly gay or lesbian staff, looking to their own attitudes with a willingness to change.[3] Attitude and behavioral change extends to supervisors, staff, and even peers in treatment (other clients, in residential settings, are powerful influences on the lesbian/ gay persons' self-esteem) as well as to other recovering individuals who are involved in such helping networks as AA. Agencies must reach out to and learn from the lesbian and gay community in their area; resources and role models must be made available to bisexual and homosexual clients. Within agencies, the climate must change so that lesbian and gay staff will be able to come out; if staff are not comfortable that they will be accepted, how then must clients feel? When we change our attitudes, we not only help those clients who enter treatment to verbalize feelings about their orientation, but we also provide an environment in which other individuals who have had homosexual feelings or experiences can be open. We thus create a climate that is healthier for us all.

We can begin to contact women's and lesbian/gay groups

in the community, establishing links with them so that they will begin to trust our agencies as resources for lesbians and gay men in need. The community is, after all, the beginning (identification and referral) and the end (resocialization, reentry, life!) of the recovery continuum. It is also a valuable resource for clients (role models, friends, lovers, supports) and staff (training and information). Most important, recovering lesbians and gay men must begin to support each other actively.

Staff members and administrators must become agents for change, learning as much as possible from the literature,[4] lesbian and gay professionals,[5] and recovering chemical abusers, even clients. Advocate where there is need, but be aware of the risk you take. You might get fired. Or, in the unfortunate Catch-22 of this issue, they might think *you* are one (that will really test your attitudes). Ultimately, when staff members work together to influence agency policy, services will be improved for all clients. At that point, it will be important to remember the world to which your clients will be returning and how much change is necessary to stop creating the problems that brought these people to you in the first place. On some level we all—administrators, staff, and clients —must begin to "treat society" in order to enhance the self-esteem of all people who are different in any way and who dare to be what they are.

**Notes**     1. Lillene Fifield, "On My Way to Nowhere, Alienated, Isolated, Drunk: An Analysis of Gay Alcohol Abuse and an Evaluation of Alcoholism Rehabilitation," a project of the Gay Community Services Center (Los Angeles: Office of Alcohol Abuse and Alcoholism, Department of Health Services, Los Angeles County, Calif., July 1975).

2. In 1977, when I worked in an Upstate New York "therapeutic community," women clients were required to wear skirts on holidays, and "faggot" and "pussy" were insult words frequently used by staff and residents alike.

3. In my agency, the executive director prohibited me from coming out to residents of the therapeutic community (clients); I could not be as open about my life as other staff members could be. I was not permitted to provide training

sessions for staff, even though we had gay residents. The director called the issue my "problem" and said we were not in the business of educating on homosexuality. When I was revealed, shortly before I left the agency, one gay client said, "I was cheated of a role model!" What message must my secrecy have conveyed?

4. Marian Sandmaier, *The Invisible Alcoholics: Women and Alcohol Abuse* (New York: McGraw-Hill Book Co., 1980); Jean Swallow, ed., *Out from Under: Sober Dykes and Our Friends* (San Francisco: Spinsters, Ink, 1983); and Thomas O. Ziebold and John E. Mongeon, *Alcoholism and Homosexuality* (New York: Haworth Press, 1982).

5. All resource materials used for this chapter are listed in the bibliography section of the Homosexuality Education and Linkage Programs (H.E.L.P.) Package by E. Sue Blume, CSW, P.O. Box 7167, Garden City, N.Y. 11530. See also "Alcoholism" in "Resources Related to Special Issues and Populations" subsection under Resources at the end of this manual.

# Some Legal Considerations in Domestic Relationships
## Kathleen Mayer

The couple entering a committed relationship may be very much in love and totally unable to think of the possibility of a breakup in the years to come. However, lesbians/gays know that such things do happen in homophile communities (just as they do in heterosexual marriages). To suggest at the outset that there might be some legal (or para-legal) contractual arrangements does not imply a sense of mistrust. It does express the concern of each for the other by making the commitment more stable. There are no laws per se that cover the relationships between two gay men or two lesbians, as there are for the couple entering a valid marriage. Therefore, such contracts not only protect each person in the event of a dissolution of the relationship, but also provide some additional protection in the event of the death of one of the partners. (See also the Schwaber chapter relative to powers of attorney and wills.) The mental health professional can be helpful to clients at any stage of the coming out process or during couple counseling by exploring the degree to which the persons can consider working with an attorney at that time or in the future. This preventative exploration is very much related to ongoing emotional well-being.

---

Laws regarding illegal sexual activity between consenting adults vary from state to state. Local communities exert some discretion and restraint as to how vigorously and under what specific circumstances they choose to enforce these laws. States also may use different precedents in making custody decisions. It is suggested that social workers become familiar with the laws controlling sexual activity in their state and the local practice regarding enforcement. State and local chapters of the American Civil Liberties Union and gay/lesbian attorneys or organizations can be useful in helping to identify and clarify specific legal issues in reference to gay men and lesbians and social work concerns.

—Editors' Note

One of the thorniest items in establishing relationships can be money and its use. Therefore, a contract should provide for identification of how income will be pooled or divided. Some indication of expectations relative to expenditures should also be included. As an adjunct to these items in a contract, an additional listing of personal property brought to the relationship should be kept. For example, keeping ongoing lists of property bought individually or jointly during the years of the relationship facilitates the keeping of insurance records and provides protection for the partners. Itemized household accounts and financial records also aid in budgeting and may prevent a need for later counseling around money-related stress.

**Relationship Contracts**

Mental health workers often hear from the client who has come for crisis intervention at the time of a severing of the relationship: "I wanted to come for counseling months ago but he/she refused." Helping the couple to agree in advance to seek outside assistance in dealing with domestic issues is another preventative measure that may lessen the potential for later turmoil. Including such a provision in a contract early in the relationship can be a way of stressing the importance of communication to both partners. The couple may even wish to stipulate which aspects of living are "negotiable" and which are "nonnegotiable" (for example, substance use/ abuse, child rearing, pets, and time with family of origin). Airing these in advance should be perceived as a plus in the self-other assessment stage.

**Counseling**

Delineating guidelines for how a dissolution of the relationship will be handled (should such a thing occur) leaves the door open for greater amicability in a breakup and can facilitate subsequent use of helping professionals during the actual breakup and afterward during the grieving process. A provision for mediating or arbitrating the issues involved in a potential dissolution can be included in a property contract. Such mediation can also ease some of the bitterness that can ensue when there is a need to work out distribution of commonly owned property, visitation or custodial rights

**Mediation or Arbitration**

related to children and even pets, or decisions about ongoing contacts with each other or with families of origin. The social worker should not view such matters as "frivolous" but should perceive them as having been extremely important during the life of the relationship and no less vital in its termination.

**Purchase of a Home** There are two possibilities here. Separate ownership is probably most practical in cases of unequal income. This should be accompanied by a contract that would provide for consideration for the nonowner in the following areas:

1. Stipulation of expected "rental payments" and their applicability to the equity in the home.

2. Decisions about the degree to which the payment is contributing to insurance costs.

3. Agreement about the amount contributed and the degree to which the nonowner is entitled to share in the tax deduction.

4. Agreement about distribution of the nonowner's share in the equity upon sale of the home or dissolution of the relationship.

Another home ownership option is that of joint tenancy with right of survivorship. This is practical when both partners are contributing equally to the costs of the home and is especially beneficial for a surviving partner in those situations where the relationship is terminated by death. However, it is necessary that there also be contractual agreements regarding what will happen to the home in the event of dissolution of the relationship. Without such a contract, legal problems can arise that will tie up the property and cause either or both partners financial hardship. Also included in this contract should be agreements relative to tax deductions, deductions for the use of the home for business purposes, and so forth.

**Conclusion** The contract can be used as a tool for facilitating clear messages about expectations and financial arrangements in a relationship. The mental health worker should be knowledgeable about community resources so that she or he can find nonhomophobic colleagues in the field of law to utilize in a team approach to the client's problems. Such a systems approach is primarily preventative in nature and may even provide for the longer life of a lesbian/gay relationship. Furthermore, the combined attorney/mental health professional involvement in this process gives social validity to the nature of the relationship in a society that all too often disregards the value of such lesbian/gay commitments.

# Some Legal Issues Related to Outside Institutions
## Fern H. Schwaber

The laws of our country and of the individual states have developed over the centuries and are designed, in part, to support and protect heterosexuality and nuclear family relationships. Because of this heterosexism, the needs of lesbians and gay men are all too often ignored in a land whose theoretical mandate is "equal protection for all." It is vital that those who provide social services be sensitized to the legal issues that lesbians and gay men must deal with in various areas of their lives.

**Illness and Admittance to Hospitals** If one becomes ill and is hospitalized, one's parents or immediate family will be accorded visitation rights, as well as participation in medical decision making. For nongays, this is often what is desired, but for lesbians or gay men, this can result in exclusion of a lover or friend. In order to ensure that one's choice for this responsibility is honored by the hospital, a medical power of attorney should be prepared. This is a legal document by which one appoints another as her or his agent with the authority to perform certain specified acts on behalf of oneself. Despite the name, there is no need for the agent to be a lawyer. Medical powers of attorney can cover a number of areas such as: visitation rights; the right to be consulted and to give or withhold consent about medical decisions; and, in case of death, the right to personal effects and the right to dispose of the body. It is advantageous for one to provide to her or his doctor and the hospital, in advance, the medical power of attorney. Gay people should be encouraged to prepare this document. For sample powers of attorney and discussions of their value, see:

> Gay Rights Task Force, *Gay Rights Skills Seminar Manual,* (2d ed.; San Francisco: National Lawyers Guild [NLG], 1979), pp. 87–89.

Hayden Curry and Denis Clifford, *A Legal Guide for Gay and Lesbian Couples* (Reading, Mass.: Addison-Wesley Publishing Co., 1980). An excellent resource book for most areas.

American Civil Liberties Union, *Lesbians and Gay Men: The Law in Pennsylvania* (Philadelphia: ACLU, 1981). An excellent resource on the law in Pennsylvania and valuable as a general text as well.

## Child Custody and Visitation Rights

When there is child custody litigation, courts more often than not award custody to the heterosexual parent, if they learn that the other parent is lesbian/gay. This has occurred regardless of the individual's ability to be an excellent parent. Fortunately, although it happens slowly, more judges are acknowledging that a parent's sexual orientation is not a reason to deny custody or visitation rights. As one judge has observed:

> Neither the prejudices of the small community in which [the children] live nor the curiosity of their peers about [the mother's] sexual nature will be abated by a change of custody....If [the mother] retains custody, it may be that because the community is intolerant of her differences these girls may sometimes have to bear themselves with greater than ordinary fortitude. But this does not necessarily portend that their moral welfare or safety will be jeopardized. It is just as reasonable to expect that they will emerge better equipped to search out their own standards of right or wrong, better able to perceive that the majority is not always correct in its moral judgments, and better able to understand the importance of conforming their beliefs to the requirements of reason and tested knowledge, not the constraints of currently popular sentiment or prejudice.
>
> Taking the children from [the mother] can be done only at the cost of sacrificing those very qualities they will find most sustaining in meeting the challenges inevitably ahead. Instead of forbearance

and feelings of protectiveness, it will foster in them a sense of shame for their mother. Instead of courage and the precept that people of integrity do not shrink from bigots, it counsels the easy option of shirking difficult problems and following the course of expedience. Lastly, it diminishes their regard for the rule of human behavior, everywhere accepted, that we do not forsake those to whom we are indebted for love and nurture merely because they are held in low esteem by others. [*M.P. v S.P.*, 404 A. 2d 1256 (N.J. Super Ct. 1979)]

In a child custody case in which the mother was a lesbian, the judge, citing from an article [Karen Gail Lewis, "Children of Lesbians: Their Point of View," *Social Work*, 25 (May 1980), pp. 198–203], held that the mother was not the best parent to have custody of her child because she was a lesbian. The court stated that this article points out that

the fact that the lesbianism of the mother, because of the failure of the community to accept and support such a condition, forces on the child a need for secrecy and the isolation imposed by such a secret, thus separating the child from his or her peers. [*S. v. S.*, 608 SW2d 64 (Ky Ct. of Appeals, 1980)]

It is unfortunate that the prejudices of others could be used to justify removing a child from a loving and caring parent. The U.S. Supreme Court, in recently holding that remarriage to a person of a different race is not sufficient to justify divesting the mother of child custody, stated,

It would ignore reality to suggest that racial and ethnic prejudices do not exist or that all manifestations of those prejudices have been eliminated. There is a risk that a child living with a stepparent of a different race may be subject to a variety of pressures and stresses not present if the child were living with parents of the same racial or ethnic origin.

The question, however, is whether the reality of private biases and the possible injury they might inflict are permissible considerations for removal of an infant child from the custody of its natural mother. We have little difficulty concluding that they are not. . . .The Constitution cannot control such prejudices but neither can it tolerate them. Private biases may be outside the reach of the law, but the law cannot, directly or indirectly, give them effect. [*Palmore v. Sidoti,* 80 L Ed 2d 421, 426 (1984)]

This reasoning is equally applicable to the homophobic prejudices that should not be a "permissible consideration" for removal of a child from the custody of its natural parent.

The emotional and psychological strain that is created by the necessity of a lesbian/gay parent's having to decide how "out" to be because of the fear of losing one's child cannot be underestimated. Decisions such as with whom to live (for example, one's lover), whether to tell the children about one's sexual orientation (children tell others), and whether to fight for alimony or child support (this might be a bargaining tool in retaining custody) are some of the issues that a parent faces.

Social workers free of homophobia can provide a great deal of support and guidance, both emotional and practical, to the lesbian/gay parent who must live with the fear of losing her or his child. Parents should be encouraged to seek out gay parent groups and lawyers for counsel. Resources include:

San Francisco–Bay Area National Lawyers Guild, Anti-Sexism Committee, *A Gay Parents' Legal Guide to Child Custody.* 2d ed., 1980). How the legal system works in custody matters; personal matters such as coming out and dealing with a spouse; and how to choose a lawyer. Address: 558 Capp St., San Francisco, Calif. 94110.

National Gay Task Force, *Gay Parent's Support Packet.* Information on child custody problems and strategies, cases won, studies of children of gays, and resources list. Address: 80 Fifth Ave., New York, N.Y. 10011.

Custody Action for Lesbian Mothers (CALM, Inc.)
P.O. Box 281
Narberth, Pa. 19072
(Litigation support service for lesbian mothers)

Gay Fathers Coalition
P.O. Box 50360
Washington, D.C. 20004

Lesbian Mothers National Defense Fund
P.O. Box 21567
Seattle, Wash. 98111

NLG *Gay Rights Skills Seminar Manual*
(cited previously)

**Immigration**   A lesbian or gay non-U.S. citizen can be refused entry to the United States because of "psychopathic personality or sexual deviance or mental defect" or because of a conviction for a crime involving "moral turpitude." Presently, the Public Health Service refuses to evaluate a person's sexual orientation for the Immigration and Naturalization Service (INS). If one does not volunteer information about her or his sexual orientation, INS officials will not ask. Recently, the Court of Appeals for the Ninth Circuit held that without the PHS evaluation a person cannot be denied entry although he admits to being gay. (*Carl Hill v. INS.*) However, once in the United States, one can be deported at any time for willful misrepresentation of a fact. If one wishes to become a permanent resident (continue to reside here, but not become a U.S. citizen), one must advise INS of all social, political, and cultural clubs and organizations that one has belonged to. If one desires to be naturalized, one must in addition be found to have "good moral character."

In a recent naturalization case involving a gay man living with his lover (*Nemetz v. INS*), the Court of Appeals for the Fourth Circuit held that one's private consensual activity cannot be the basis for a finding of lack of "good moral character" and thereby a denial of a petition for naturalization. Lesbians and gays concerned about obtaining visas, deportation, or being naturalized should consult lawyers who specialize in immigration law. Gay legal organizations, such as

Lambda Legal Defense and Education Fund, Inc. (for address, see list of legal rights organizations in Resources), American Civil Liberties Union (ACLU), and the National Lawyers Guild (NLG, a politically progressive legal organization) may be able to provide resources.

**Wills**

Each state has its laws for regulating the distribution of one's property after death. If a person dies without leaving a will, the property is distributed according to the "intestacy" law, which divides property based on traditional familial relationships. Written wills, therefore, are important because they allow one to leave property to whomever she or he chooses, rather than just to those specified by the state legislature. Because of the tragic consequences that may result (the deceased's relatives successfully obtaining property that the deceased thought would go to a lover), lesbians and gays should be encouraged to write wills. Local bookstores usually provide do-it-yourself manuals. Other resources include:

> NLG *Gay Rights Skills Seminar Manual* (cited previously)
>
> Curry and Clifford, *A Legal Guide for Gay and Lesbian Couples* (cited previously)

Depending on the laws of the state concerned and the complexity of the individual's estate, consultation with a lawyer may be appropriate.

**Criminal Law**

A number of states have statutes that make it a criminal offense to engage in homosexual practices, both publicly and privately. Penalties vary, but usually include jail sentences. Within those states that have these laws, enforcement practices vary. Some agencies still lure gay men with police decoys; others merely arrest those engaging in sexual acts in public places (e.g., an empty bathroom in the Capitol building). A number of state courts have held that such statutes, which usually reflect community prejudices, violate constitutional standards. Those who are convicted of sodomy or "crimes against nature" statutes may be barred from entering certain professional fields or from being employed because they are considered convicted felons. Anyone who has such a conviction from a state that has since overturned the statute, should consult a lawyer (including the local public defender's office), about getting the conviction removed from the criminal record.

**Licensure**   Each state has its own regulations requiring licensing of individuals engaged in various professions. Often before a person is licensed, an inquiry is made into her or his personal character. A conviction for violating a state law (for example, a consensual sodomy statute) can be a basis for denial of a license. It is important for gay people to ascertain whether one's sexual orientation could be the basis for denial of a license. This information can be obtained from gay organizations as well as from the professional organization representing the particular profession.

**Private Employment**   No one has the right to a job in the private sector. Generally, an employer may fire an employee at any time, for any or no reason. Lesbians and gays have been fired from their jobs merely because of their sexuality. However, if the state or local government prohibits discrimination in employment of the basis of sexual orientation, then gay people are protected from this form of discrimination. Some employers include a nondiscrimination clause, including sexual orientation, in their personnel manuals. Some union contracts provide similar protection. Social service providers should be familiar with the laws of their locality and state regarding discrimination. The National Gay Task Force has published a brochure on private employers who have nondiscrimination policies (NGTF address cited previously).

**AIDS**   AIDS (Acquired Immune Deficiency Syndrome) appears to be a new disorder. It renders the body's immune or defense system incapable of adequately fighting off infections that would not normally affect healthy individuals. The portion of the immune system most affected by this is the cell-mediated immune system and is characterized by a diminished number of thymus-dependent lymphocytes.

The AIDS deficiency itself is a silent condition that predisposes the affected individual to a number of opportunistic processes including Kaposi's sarcoma (KS), Pneumocystis carinii pneumonia (PCP), central nervous system toxoplasmosis, disseminated cytomegalovirus infection, intractable herpes-simplex virus infections, and lymphoproliferative disorders among others. At present there is no known cure or effective tratement for the immune deficiency itself. The outlook for people who have it is extremely guarded.

Federal disability benefits are available to people with AIDS. Social services providers should become familiar with the procedures and eligibility requirements for attaining benefits. Unfortunately, the AIDS crisis has resulted in discrimination in employment and in the delivery of health care services to people with AIDS. However, although there is a dearth of legislation protecting gay people, there is federal as well as local legislation in most states prohibiting discrimination on the basis of disability. Such legislation has been a successful tool in fighting discrimination against people with AIDS. Resources include:

Gay Men's Health Crisis, Inc.
P.O. Box 274
132 W. 24th St.
New York, N.Y. 10011

*AIDS Legal Guide: A Professional Resource on AIDS-Related Issues and Discrimination*
Lambda Legal Defense and Education Fund, Inc.
132 W. 43rd St.
New York, N.Y. 10036

# Crisis Intervention and Suicide Counseling with Gay and Lesbian Clients
## Christian A. Frandsen

**Issues and Problem Areas**

Crisis intervention with any client involves a particularly knowledgeable, comprehensive, and compassionate model of practice. Because of the unique and widespread misunderstanding, prejudice, and discrimination affecting most gays and lesbians, crisis work with these clients often demands an even more sensitive and informed approach.

The acute state of distress experienced by clients in crisis frequently renders their usual external as well as intrapersonal support systems dysfunctional. The client feels confused, alienated, and powerless. A client experiencing suicidal ideation is usually in an especially profound state of anguish. Denial of self-worth and value are common. Overwhelming feelings of despair, helplessness, and hopelessness are almost always manifested. For a gay or lesbian client engulfed in such a situation, the trauma can be greatly exacerbated by perceived and actual oppression by society, family, and peers. When the client is still "closeted," the very fear of discovery can precipitate a crisis. Thus, the variable of a homosexual orientation can be an important consideration even though it is not the actual presenting problem.

Research and experience have indicated that most gay or lesbian clients do not usually seek crisis counseling solely because of problems directly attributable to their sexual orientation. Rather, gay men or lesbians seek such services for life-stress situations like those experienced by nongay clients. Acute interpersonal relationship difficulties, feelings of social isolation, chronic depression, personal and economic loss, serious illness, and a myriad of other circumstances precipitate crises for gay and nongay individuals alike. However, the added factor of a client's gay/lesbian orientation can compound a crisis because of the limited support systems available. Unfortunately, this paucity of resources may include the small number of empathetic and informed helping professionals.

Crisis intervention with gay or lesbian clients necessitates an honest, supportive, nonjudgmental, and nonpatronizing attitude. If the client's sexual orientation is not considered by him or her to be a relevant factor in the crisis, it should not become a focal point. If the client and worker do identify that gayness or lesbianism is pertinent, only those aspects directly relevant to the intervention should be examined. Crisis intervention does not and should not allow for overexpansion or overdevelopment of issues. Neither the worker nor the client should be permitted to drift from the focal and emergent problems. Evasion or neglect of the presenting issues can preclude problem resolution and may lead to intensification or repetition of the crisis. Follow-up or special sessions are more suitable for examination of secondary concerns. **Interventive Strategies**

Clients should always be supported in the positive aspects of their lifestyle and individuality, and they must be reassured that they are not to blame for societal hatred, persecution, or exclusion based on homophobia. The client must be helped not to internalize such negativism. To do so can lead to the addition of various short- and long-term problems.

Reality-based answers and action alternatives are essential. The worker needs to be honest, empathic, clear, and concise throughout the intervention. If there is a particular concern or confusion during the session, it should be addressed immediately. And, the worker should ascertain that the client is clear about what is needed and expected during and after the session.

In working with chronically stressed or suicidal clients, the guidelines listed above can be crucial. There are some other basic points to keep in mind as well. The suicide rate is highest among males, especially those age 50 or more; suicide is also a major cause of death among adolescents. If the client has made a previous suicide attempt, or if an actual suicide plan has been developed, the likelihood of an actual attempt is greater. If the crisis intervention is to take place over the phone on a "hot line," the worker should stay alert for signs of heightened nervousness or depression, for slurred or significantly slowed speech patterns, and for background sounds; the caller may decide to take some pills or otherwise harm himself or herself during the call. If the caller is not willing or is unable to talk at some point (for example, because of nervousness, crying, and so forth), he or she should be reassured that the worker will remain on the line and be available to assist when the caller is ready. At some point, it can also be useful to lead the caller in some quick relaxation exercises if there seems to be heightened agitation. In any case, what is often most necessary is for the worker to be an empathic and warm *listener;* the last thing that is needed is a preachy, punitive, *lecturer.*

A significant part of crisis counseling involves acting as a resource or referral source for follow-up work. After virtually every crisis intervention, there is need for some sort of auxiliary service. The crisis worker should be well aware of special community support systems available to gay/lesbian clients. Although the client needs to be encouraged to develop self-help skills and independence, the worker may need to initiate some calls or appointments on behalf of the client. A final and very definite responsibility of a crisis worker is to be an active advocate for clients—or potential clients—in the development and implementation of support systems and legislation designed to serve gay and lesbian persons and to decrease significantly the special crises attributable to a homophobic response to their sexual orientation.

# Social Growth Groups for Lesbians and Gays
## Harry R. Lenna

**A** group setting can offer special value when working with **Introduction**
gays and lesbians who have essentially accepted their
same-sex orientation but wish to explore that identification
more fully in its personal and social implications. Many such
clients, particularly those in the early stages of coming out,
may be in positions of considerable social isolation. Interacting with a diverse group of others who share their same-sex
affectional orientation can be, in itself, socially satisfying and
reinforcing to the participants' sense of self-worth.

There is no single gay or lesbian lifestyle. Diversity of
personalities and lifestyles among participants in a group can
offer a setting that stimulates thoughtful and individualized
development of self-definition while, at the same time, encourages understanding and acceptance of the diversity to be
found in the homosexual community. The ongoing interaction with others of shared purpose, but differing views and
patterns of social behavior, can enhance the sense of support and shared identity.

There are a number of stressful or problem areas to which **Issues and**
participants of such a social growth group may want to direct **Problems**
their attention. Participants should be encouraged to verbalize their personal concerns as a part of the initial stages of
the development of basic group cohesion. A goal of these
initial meetings is to create comfort among group members
in discussing their perceptions of their homosexuality openly.
Group facilitators should not be surprised if tensions arise
due to discomfort with differences in self-concepts and social
behaviors that may be expressed. As in any social growth
group, the facilitator would stress and work to establish principles of mutual respect and the desire to understand diversity. Appropriate and critical judgment of other members'

**103**

self-understanding and resultant choices of behavior demands these underlying principles of respect and understanding.

Gays and lesbians who have felt some sense of undefined stress about their sexual-affectional identification are often those who are unable to offer more than a very narrow self-definition of their gayness or lesbianism. If the facilitator finds that such a narrow self-definition characterizes a significant number in the group, it is suggested that this problem become the next area for group exploration. The goal of these group sessions should be the clarification and expansion of a personal and positive sense of self that can provide a better basis for moving away from residual reactive responses and toward appropriately assertive and proactive behavior that serves to affirm a lesbian or gay identification. From the perspective of a lesbian identification, the book edited by Vida, *Our Right to Love,* offers an excellent resource to facilitators and group participants.[1] Clark's *Loving Someone Gay* offers valuable insight into the issues of defining oneself as gay.[2] Woodman and Lenna, in *Counseling with Gay Men and Women,* have focused on a number of issues that are likely to be raised at all stages of the group's efforts.[3]

A gay or lesbian identification finds its validation in action. When the individual has developed a clearer and more specific definition of self, it can be expected that he or she will have an enhanced need for validation. This forms the next level of issues on which participants often desire to focus attention. Living a lifestyle that, in some degree or other, presents open acknowledgment and affirmation of one's homosexuality carries with it inevitable social implications and problems. Social validation demands that gays and lesbians find appropriate contexts and opportunities where they can act in keeping with their sense of self. Unfortunately, given the still largely homophobic nature of society, rejection or only qualified acceptance can often be the response of others. For a wide variety of reasons, coming out to others may have to be selective. Personal decision making in this regard can form an important group activity at this stage. Varied strategies for dealing with different social contexts may be necessary. Books that can be very helpful resource reading include *Living Gay* by Clark and, for lesbians, *The Coming Out Stories,* edited by Stanley and Wolfe.[4]

Don't promote the group as therapy. Both because of previous experiences with change-oriented therapists and knowledge or heresay about such experiences in others, many lesbians or gays who might otherwise participate may have a negative reaction if the group is called "therapy."

Do establish groups in traditional or neutral settings. Many gays and lesbians may not be ready for, or for any of a number of other reasons, may feel they cannot make use of, opportunities sponsored by lesbian and gay centers.

Do make a careful assessment of whether the primary felt need of group members is coming to terms with oneself as homosexual or is more focused on the social aspects of a lesbian or gay identification. Although overlap exists between these stages of coming out, each can present quite different problems that need exploration. It may prove desirable to form two groups if circumstances permit. If not, then the facilitator will need to guide group discussions so that both issue areas receive appropriate consideration.

Often gender-segregated groups have been found efficacious. This is *not* because of the old myth that lesbians hate men and gays hate women. Rather, because of different socialization patterns and the pragmatics of life situations, gays and lesbians face different types of problems and different private and social orientations to similar problems. In those instances where circumstances demand a gender-integrated group, it is highly recommended that a male and female team of facilitators work together.

Know and be able to refer clients/participants to other gay and lesbian resources and support contexts outside the growth group itself. Most larger urban areas have a wide variety of such resources already existing. Contact with a local gay and lesbian center can give you needed information about types of groups, their meeting places, and contact persons. In less populated areas, informal social networking among gays and lesbians may exist. Your group should not become an end in itself but rather a means to a more fulfilling, proactive lifestyle.

Don't focus only on comparisons to heterosexual lifestyles. Gay and lesbian clients will be far more interested in searching out, understanding, and finding positive confirmation of what makes them unique and how to find fulfillment within their own unique identification and lifestyles.

Don't press participants toward a group agenda that is too heavily or too quickly focused on the "I." In the earlier stages, more comfort is often found in focusing on the "we" of a shared identification.

Do be open and frank about your own sexual-affectional identification, whatever that may be. Lack of candor by the facilitator can inhibit candor among participants.

**Notes**   1. Ginny Vida, ed., *Our Right to Love: A Lesbian Resource Book* (Englewood Cliffs, N.J.: Prentice-Hall, 1978).

2. Don Clark, *Loving Someone Gay* (New York: New American Library, Signet Books, 1977).

3. Natalie Jane Woodman and Harry R. Lenna, *Counseling with Gay Men and Women: A Guide for Facilitating Positive Life-Styles* (San Francisco: Jossey-Bass, 1980).

4. Don Clark, *Living Gay* (Millbrae, Calif.: Celestial Arts Publishing Co., 1979); and Julia Penelope Stanley and Susan J. Wolfe, eds., *The Coming Out Stories* (Watertown, Mass.: Persephone Press, 1980).

# Residential Treatment for Youth
## Pat Terry

Twenty-four-hour treatment is the claim and foundation of residential programs. Participants in such programs are continually observed by staff members and scrutinized by peers. The complexities of adolescence can be intensified in such settings because social and sexual behaviors are often the focus of treatment. Adolescents are subjected to enormous internal and external stress as they seek to find and identify themselves. It is often difficult to determine if affectional and sexual preference during adolescence is transitional, experimental, or, in fact, a lifestyle.

Historical and present-day attitudes toward same-gender affectional and sexual preference are perhaps more honestly expressed by youth. Venomous exchanges of "faggot" and "queer" are frequently heard in residential programs. Defending oneself against such allegations can become an adolescent goal. The external peer pressure is certainly significant enough for any teenager. One must then consider the adolescent who is in a residential program because of severe emotional disturbance and who then experiences social and sexual behaviors and thoughts that clearly indicate same-gender preference. The internal stress in combination with family, peer, and—unfortunately—staff attitudes can be intolerable. It is very probable that gender preference will become an overriding factor in the treatment approach and in the therapeutic intervention. In addition, progress in treatment may be measured by the individual's ability to modify same-gender preference to the more "acceptable" opposite-gender attraction. Families will be happier and staff certainly will take credit for exceptional role modeling and expert intervention during this critical "identity crisis." The client may also show signs of being "less disturbed" and more satisfied with his or her life. Once again, "choosing" the conventional gender preference has resolved external conflict and "cured the primary problem."

**Stress Reduction** The observed changes are more likely to be a result of stress reduction through accommodation rather than a "cure" through changing gender attraction. It is highly likely that the internal stress has only been capped and will surface again unless the individual was just experiencing transitional feelings and behaviors. The unfortunate result of stress reduction through accommodation is that the next time gender preference conflict arises, a marriage and children can be involved.

Stress reduction is a viable interventive technique. Treatment staff in residential settings can effectively use such methodologies because of the amount of environmental control and influence that exists in such programs for youth. Many staff members are as uncomfortable in dealing with same-gender preference as are families and the individual in treatment. Training staff in demonstrating accepting attitudes and examining their own homophobic values is much too simplistic for this situation, but cannot be overlooked as a strategy for improving the treatment setting. Hiring staff who have same-gender preference and who then can provide healthy role modeling behaviors is methodologically sound but usually as "unthinkable" for program development as is coming out in the work situation for staff members.

When one works with youth, caution must always be exercised. This is a vulnerable developmental stage, and making assumptions about an individual's gender preference is clinically unsound. Directing or steering youth toward one or another preference is a "no win" approach. The adolescent needs to be aware of the right to choose and to be allowed to exercise self-determination. Stress reduction is essential, but not at the price of accommodation. External stress can be decreased through support from family, peers, and staff. The internal stress, although modified by external factors, must also be addressed.

**What Can Be Done** There is a monumental difference between what should be done and what can be done in residential settings for youth as it relates to gender preference. As discussed previously, role modeling by self-actualizing adult staff with lesbian/gay identities is an approach. Congruent with this is work with families and significant others to facilitate their acceptance of such a lifestyle so that they can ultimately support the adolescent. Exposure to youth groups and organizations for parents and friends of gays would decrease feelings of isolation and possible inferiority. This positive approach is often opposed by administrators and homophobic supervisory staff. The policy in regard to lesbian and gay issues adopted by the National Association of Social Workers and other professional organizations can be useful in providing a "professional base" of support toward implementing this positive approach to lesbian and gay youth in residential treatment. As a bare minimum, clinicians must provide the support and information that will lead to family and individual acceptance of the lesbian or gay adolescent's lifestyle, in place of a perception of the situation as "pathological functioning."

# SECTION II
## Macro Intervention

# Introduction
Hilda Hidalgo

The title of "social worker" has often been interchanged with that of "agent of social change." Many will argue that in spite of our heritage and our public ethical commitment to change dehumanizing institutional practices and attitudes, the social work profession has often acted as an "agent of social control." The efforts of social workers to intervene at the macro level have often taken a secondary position, and our energies have been directed for the most part at making individuals "adapt" to oppressive situations. This has been particularly true in relation to the oppression of lesbians and gay men.

A major thrust of the efforts of the users of this manual should be directed at strategies to change legislation, business, the media, and human services systems that so often oppress gay men and lesbians. To do this effectively, political activism and sophistication are necessary tools. It is also essential that our strategies include coalitions with other organizations interested in gay/lesbian issues and willing to be helpful (see Resources for partial list of organizations in this category).

# Model for Institutional Change
## Bernice Goodman

To accomplish institutional change takes persistence, leadership, and organization. Institutions are supported and maintained by a network of complementary organizations in the society. This network of organizations has deeply rooted homophobic policies and practices. Organizations, particularly the ones closely related to social work practice, must be targeted for change. Three distinct phases in the effort to formulate and direct change strategies and facilitate evaluation of the change effort at each phase have been identified and diagramed. We will use the experience of the National Association of Social Workers (NASW) with the issue of lesbian and gay rights as an example of this model in practice.

**Initial Phase** The initial phase focuses on identifying the organization targeted for change, organizing the change agent resources, and evaluating and assessing the organization targeted for change. (See Fig. 1.) The work necessary to effect the NASW public policy statement in 1979 re lesbian and gay rights began in the early 1970s. The change agents in this initial phase were scattered throughout the country and were inhibited by the "closet attitude" of most professional social workers. This was matched by the formal structures and informal attitudes of NASW and other professional groups. Change began to occur when a small group of professionals, such as Ron Lee and the author, began giving papers, requesting space at conferences, and holding meetings and caucuses of any lesbian and gay social workers who would risk attending. This process began in 1970, and each year continued to grow.

**Middle Phase** The middle phase focuses on implementing the change strategies in a systematic effort of asserting pressure according to a plan that ranks actions for change. It begins when the

114

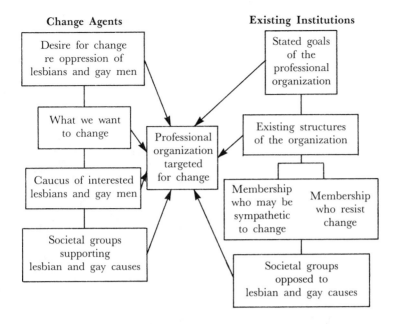

**Change Agents**

Desire for change re oppression of lesbians and gay men

What we want to change

Caucus of interested lesbians and gay men

Societal groups supporting lesbian and gay causes

Professional organization targeted for change

**Existing Institutions**

Stated goals of the professional organization

Existing structures of the organization

Membership who may be sympathetic to change

Membership who resist change

Societal groups opposed to lesbian and gay causes

FIGURE 1. INITIAL PHASE

targeted organization has recognized specific behaviors, policies, or procedures that need to be changed and the change agents have worked out a working relationship with the organization targeted. Leadership in the change agency group has been identified and is working effectively. (See Fig. 2.)

This middle phase is most crucial because the targets for change need to be identified both individually and collectively as well as simultaneously. For example, in relation to NASW the change agents (stated goals of the members of NASW re lesbian and gay issues) did not exist. We, lesbian and gay members, had to begin to translate general stated goals of NASW as these, by logic, applied to lesbian and gay people. We worked closely with NASW national staff, and they supported us to attend the 1977 Delegate Assembly in Portland, Oregon. Once this work was accom-

Figures 1–3 are adapted from Bernice Goodman, ''Where Will You Be?'' *The Professional Oppression of Gay People: A Lesbian/Feminist Perspective* (West Hempstead, N.Y.: Woman Made Products, 1980), pp. 20–22.

**Model for Institutional Change     115**

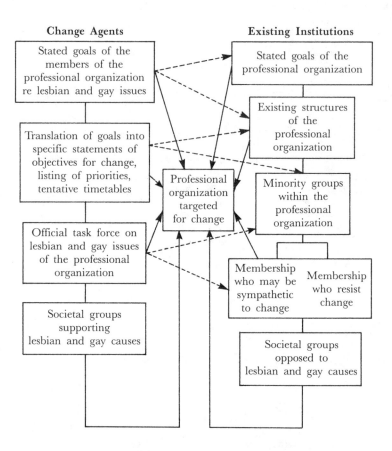

Change Agents

Existing Institutions

FIGURE 2. MIDDLE PHASE

plished, we identified specific goals and objects for change. The next step was to establish priorities that would move us to "real" change—not just to a state of "token" change.

This change is most clearly understood related to the public policy statement passed in the delegate assembly in Portland (see Appendix B). At first, delegates only wanted to pass the statement and not require a follow-up mechanism. However, those of us working on passing the statement were clear that it would be relatively useless without a mandated structure to implement the policy. With this in mind, we insisted on the establishment of a National Task Force on Lesbian and Gay Issues as an integral part of the policy statement. Almost two years later through constant and persistent pressure, we held the first meeting of this task force. These sessions became the firm base from which NASW would be held accountable to recognize and meet the needs of its lesbian and gay members. In addition, NASW had to begin to recognize the large lesbian and gay client group that were not being served properly because of homophobic attitudes of social workers and organizations.

At the first task force meeting, we contacted many local and regional lesbian and gay social workers to meet with us. Many people from all parts of the country attended at their own expense. Where we had been "none," now we were "many." Each person returned to his or her part of the country and began to work with various local organizations and local chapters of NASW.

Simultaneously, we were requesting and pressuring the national staff to include and support lesbian and gay concerns. Gradually, we became more visible and gained more support from members of NASW who were not lesbian or gay. In addition, the structures for conferences, public statements, and staff planning included lesbian and gay issues without encountering too much resistance.

In this middle phase of change, visibility is the essential keystone. Visibility makes it hard to continue to ignore lesbian and gay issues, and people who are not lesbian or gay begin to accept "our" issues as "theirs."


**Final Phase**

The final phase focuses on the institutionalization of humanistic and pluralistic values and practices visible in the day-to-day functioning of the organization. In this phase, the organization that initially was targeted for change becomes involved in the change effort of other organizations. The individual change agents and the organization as an entity target other organizations in the social service network. The change cycle begins anew with another organization targeted for change. (See Fig. 3.)

In this final phase, we have to be careful that members and the NASW organization do not become "bored" and begin to ignore lesbian and gay issues. There is a tendency to assume that some amount of change has occurred and that is enough. The roles of the task force and other newly

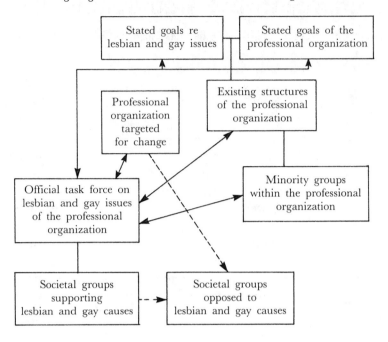

Change Agents                              Existing Institutions

FIGURE 3. FINAL PHASE

established professional groups dedicated to lesbian and gay issues are crucial at this time. They must be the assertive advocates of these issues. They must monitor the actions of NASW to assure that change becomes institutionalized and new issues are addressed as they arise. For example, the recent AIDS epidemic clearly establishes homophobia as the basic social disease that accounts for the neglect and negative manner in which this health issue has been handled.

It is the constant surveillance, action, movement, and grass-roots connections that make this model for change a vibrant, effective system. Built into this system is the need for constant reevaluation of issues and constant action. It is a system that facilitates change in the most difficult situations.

118    Model for Institutional Change

# Changing the Traditional Human Service Agency on Behalf of Lesbian and Gay Male Clients
## Ron Balint

A primary problem in social service delivery to lesbian/gay people is the unwillingness of traditional service providers to respond to the special needs of these clients. Following are several ways of gaining leverage and causing traditional agencies to provide needed services. The premise behind this material is that although lesbian/gay communities can deliver some services, they can never provide the full gamut of social services needed and, as a result, traditional agencies must be encouraged to serve a lesbian/gay population.

Although the first two steps in moving a traditional agency to provide services to lesbian/gay people are self-evident, we include them for the sake of being complete.

1. Identify and spell out the need, as you see it, as specifically as possible; for example, there is a significant need for group work with recovering lesbian alcoholics.

2. Answer the key question of which agency, if any, is able to fill the need through a service delivery plan.

After you have identified the need and located an appropriate agency able to do the service delivery plan, your next step is to bring the agency from not only being able, but also to being willing to fill the need. There are a host of ways to bring this about. Following are some ways that have been tried and found workable. It is important for the reader to recognize that there is no set blueprint, but that basically any combination of the following techniques can be used.

After determining which agency can fill a specified gap, you must determine which persons are in a position to bring about your service delivery plan. This person needs to get your message from as many different sources as possible. These sources ought to be both internal to the agency and external. They might include:

*Internal:* other lesbian/gay employees
nonlesbian/nongay people who are sympathetic employees
persons who might gain by this service delivery plan (e.g., a social service department)
board of directors' members
community advisory board members

*External:* other agencies
clients/consumers
contributors
unions
professional organizations
persons in an auditing or utilization review position

It is important that not only the general message gets through ("Do something for lesbian/gay people") but also that a more specific message be communicated ("Recovering alcoholic lesbian women have no support/therapy groups available to them"). The more specific message need come from only a few of your message carriers.

**Service Delivery Plan** Once the above messages have been received, the person in the position to authorize a service delivery plan should be contacted and presented with a potential plan. An outlined plan presented in an orderly fashion will maximize your success potential. Knowing an agency's written mission and any nondiscriminatory statements made by the agency is vital to your presentation and should be included in it. It is both appropriate and important for leverage to help an administrator remember that your plan is, for example, "in keeping with the agency's mission to serve the whole community," or is "a direct outgrowth of the policy statement on nondiscrimination in service provision." It might also be helpful to remind an administrator that a particular plan is in response to the attitudes expressed by a particular professional organization or union in their lesbian/gay policy statement.

The service delivery plan itself should have a maximum chance of success. The original plan should be modest in scope and unquestionably doable. If at all possible, there should be funding available apart from that that the agency doing the service might provide. It is also helpful to have a time frame for the project. An administrator is much more likely to commit an agency to a project that:

- appears logically workable,

- will cost a minimum amount,

- is small enough so that if it fails, the agency will not have its public image tarnished,

- is time limited so that if it flounders or if there are unforeseen problems, it can be permitted to "die a natural death" as opposed to being cancelled.

It is more probable that an agency will sponsor a therapy group for lesbian alcoholics, meeting weekly for seven weeks, meeting after regular working hours, with time volunteered by a professional therapist, than give a commitment to "provide ongoing services to a lesbian recovering alcoholic population." The suggestion of starting small is not intended to convey being satisfied with crumbs from the table—but it is significantly easier to build on one success and expand its scope than to package and sell an entire program.

A long-range plan divided into increments will maximize one's potential for success. It is vital for one to realize that a therapy group for lesbian recovering alcoholics would take a different form administratively if it were a first step in developing a lesbian-oriented detox unit than if it were a first step toward funding community-based support-group networks.

The principles involved in gaining leverage and influencing **Perspective** change in social service agencies are no different for pro lesbian/gay changes than they would be for most other changes benefiting a minority. Homophobia will be a primary obstacle but the principles remain the same. If a plan is sloppy, poorly developed, and not thought out, it will be rejected by an administrator. Such rejection is not necessarily homophobic, and the charge of homophobia should not be made as an excuse for shoddy work. Homophobia is real and needs to be dealt with as such—it is not an acceptable excuse for poor work. It is neither an imaginary element to be dismissed, nor is it an unsurmountable barrier. Realistically understanding how homophobia affects one's work is necessary for success.

In summary, one of the most important elements in one's work is perspective. When trying to bring influence to bear for a service delivery plan, an advocate is not begging that something be graciously given, but is rather advocating for something to which a population is entitled. Having one's "act together" regarding lesbian/gay issues gives a perspective that nothing else can compensate for. It is a prerequisite for doing a quality piece of advocacy.

# SECTION III

## Professional Relationships and Professional Development

# Introduction
## Hilda Hidalgo

In-service training, continuing education activities, and administrative and personnel policies that center on lesbian/gay issues must be a top priority if the NASW policy on gay and lesbian issues is going to be more than a paper declaration for lesbian/gay rights. It is important that agency administrators attend and encourage staff attendance at workshops, seminars, and institutes related to gay and lesbian issues. Whenever possible, compensatory time should be provided for the workers in order to encourage and enable them to participate in these activities, and arrangements to grant continuing education credit to participants should be secured.

The education of social workers at the undergraduate and graduate level has at best avoided the issues related to lesbian/gay oppression and at worse contributed to this oppression. Professional development and education must therefore now include corrective learning and deprogramming for the social worker whose knowledge, values, and practice behaviors are the result of a homophobic knowledge base and value system. This section and the Appendixes that follow it include materials and suggestions that will help to provide such training.

# Administrative, Personnel, and Professional Policies of Social Work Agencies and Institutions: Lesbian and Gay Issues
## Hilda Hidalgo

**A**ll social work agencies and institutions include in their personnel policies statements that they do not discriminate on the basis of race, religion, national origin, and sex. A few also include age and physical handicaps in their discrimination disclaimer. Fewer still include *sexual orientation* in their statements. The time has come for all agencies to do so.

**Sexual** The lack of an antidiscrimination policy based on sexual
**Orientation** orientation has forced lesbians and gays to remain invisible, to channel a portion of their energies into living double lives, and to live in constant fear of losing their jobs—or not getting jobs—because of their sexual orientation. In many ways, lesbians and gays in the closet are in a position similar to the one that "passing blacks" were in prior to the civil rights acts and the black civil rights movement. The fact that many lesbians and gay male social workers are "in the closet" reinforces the belief that there are few, if any, lesbians and gay men on the staffs of social service agencies.

All discriminated-against minority groups know that an "equal opportunity statement" does not necessarily mean that the agency or institution honors in practice its antidiscrimination statement. However, oppressed minority groups agree that such a statement is useful and necessary in order to: (1) prevent blatant discrimination; (2) encourage members of the minority groups to test the implementation of the statement; and (3) begin a process of education and change in the institution or agency and in the community at large.

The policy statement adopted by NASW in reference

to lesbian and gay issues (see Appendixes A and B) makes it possible to bring to the consciousness of institutions and agencies the need to include "sexual orientation" in antidiscriminatory personnel policy statements. The NASW policy statement also gives social workers the professional sanction and ethical responsibility to advocate actively for the inclusion of sexual orientation in antidiscriminatory policy statements. Following NASW's lead, the Council on Social Work Education adopted Evaluation Standards 11 (Undergraduate) and 12 (Graduate) barring accredited programs in social work education from discriminating on the basis of sexual orientation (see Appendix C).

All agencies and institutions have a body of procedures that, while not included in their personnel statements, are nonetheless part of the "informal personnel policies and practices" that create a positive work climate and contribute to employees' morale. Such practices include agency-related social occasions such as annual picnics, holiday parties and dinners, and wedding showers, as well as the sending of flowers or cards when an employee's spouse or close family member is in the hospital. Many agency-related social occasions recognize the desirability of the employees including "the significant other" in their personal life in these occasions. Spouses, fiancees, or opposite-sex friends are therefore explicitly included in the invitations to agency-sponsored official and "unofficial" social events. It should be a given that lesbian and gay employees have the same consideration and that their "significant others" are welcomed and included in such social occasions.

Large institutions and agencies have employees' unions that negotiate with the administration on working conditions, policies related to personnel benefits, and so on. It is important to work within the union structure for the inclusion, in the binding contractual agreement, of an antidiscriminatory clause protecting lesbian/gay workers. Unions and other professional organizations have been known to be receptive to including lesbians/gays in their antidiscriminatory clauses— for example, the Rutgers University chapter of the Association of American University Professors included such a clause in their contract with the university years before CSWE advocated such a provision in the accreditation standards.

An antidiscriminatory statement that includes sexual orientation, however, is of relatively little value if the climate and day-to-day practices of the agency or institution make it very difficult for lesbian and gay workers to be professionally "out of the closet." An even more positive approach is to seek actively (an affirmative action stance) openly gay and lesbian social workers and staff to apply for vacancies. If one considers that at least 10 percent of the population is lesbian or gay, one can legitimize the desirability of social work agencies investing at least as much effort in the recruitment, retention, promotion, and visibility of lesbian and gay social workers and staff as they do in the recruitment, retention, promotion, and visibility of the other oppressed minorities included in their antidiscriminatory statements.

**Lesbian and Gay Couples**  Unfortunately, discrimination, bigotry, and homophobia deny lesbian and gay individuals and couples in a primary relationship many of the same benefits and rights that heterosexual couples in a primary relationship enjoy and take for granted. Personnel policies of agencies usually include personal leave days and spell out the situations for which personal leave is granted. Common practice is to mention such things as death or serious illness of a close family member and other family crisis situations. Lesbian and gay couples should be recognized by agencies as a primary family unit and should be given equal consideration in the granting of personal leave in relation to "family situations."

Lesbian and gay couples also cannot take advantage of group health insurance rates that agencies make available to the "spouse" and children of a heterosexual primary relationship. We recognize that, at the present time, there is little that agencies can do to change the policies of health insurance companies and of other companies (for instance, life insurance, travel discounts, and so forth) that make it possible for agencies to provide important fringe benefits to their employees. However, we should call attention to such discriminatory practices as a first step in advocating their change.

The following steps should be implemented in order to eliminate discrimination against lesbians and gays by social work agencies and institutions.

1. Agencies' and institutions' personnel policies, employees' contracts, and official and unofficial practices should be scrutinized to determine to what degree they discriminate in conscious or unconscious ways against lesbian and gay employees and clients.

2. A prioritized list of actions and strategies with a projected timetable should be spelled out and implemented in order to correct all forms of discrimination against lesbians and gays—be these a result of acts of commission or omission. *Blatant* discriminatory policies and procedures should be eliminated posthaste.

3. Agencies guilty of blatant discrimination and unwilling to take corrective actions should be reported, and sanctions against them should be taken by NASW.

## NASW Professional Policies in Relation to Lesbian and Gay Issues

The *NASW Compilation of Social Policy Statements* (September 1983) lists all adoptions by this organization since 1963. In light of the policy on gay issues (1977—see Appendix B) and of the issues and concerns raised by the authors in Section I (Populations at Risk) of this resource manual, several policy statements need to be revised to include the special concerns of lesbians and gay men. As currently written, there is a definite heterosexist assumption underlying the policies on children, families, health care, and aging—to mention only a few. (The extent of the revisions needed is beyond the scope of this resource manual.)

An example of how these policies need to be updated to reflect sensitivity to lesbians and gays can be found in the policy statement on aging, where there is a section that addresses minority elderly. Lesbians and gays are indeed a minority population, yet their needs are not addressed in this policy nor by most aging programs that are developed by the heterosexual elderly. Enlightened social workers can begin making such modifications and inclusions in interpreting and implementing NASW's policy statements.

Policies are guides for action, and it is time that the actions of social workers and their professional practices reflect respect, concern, and consideration for the needs of lesbians and gay men—be they clients or colleagues.

# Coming Out in Social Work: Worker Survival, Support, and Success
## John Grace

**C**oming out—identifying, understanding, and respecting one's homosexuality and disclosing this positive identity to others—is an enormously complex and idiosyncratic process. Yet, while each coming out story is ultimately a uniquely personal searching for self and community, many commonalities and similar patterns of identity development emerge when different people's experiences are shared.

The following thoughts and observations on what it is like to come out as an individual and a social worker derive from these commonalities. This shared history provides a panorama on the myriad hardships, struggles, and successes of gay and lesbian people who are simply trying to be themselves in a society that still frequently responds with fear, hatred, and punishment to any individual or group it deems different.

**Coming Out as a Process: The Stages** Rather than a single event or short-term series of events, coming out is a lifelong developmental process containing a number of important stages and life tasks. In my work, I use a five-stage model developed in collaboration with gay and lesbian colleagues.[1] Briefly the stages are as follows:

1. *Emergence* explores the beginning awareness of "difference" in the individual and its growing influence on behavior, self-concept, family dynamics, and peer relations;

2. *Acknowledgment* begins when the individual attempts to understand and cope with homoerotic feelings and self-identification;

3. *Finding community* is a search for peer groups and social milieux in which gay and lesbian identity is openly expressed and respected;

4. *Building relationships* may be complicated by negative myths and stereotypes about homosexuality as well as a lack of positive role models for personal and professional relationships;

5. *Self-definition and reintegration* describe the continuing establishment of a positive and proactive self-concept, one that is not defined in ignorance and isolation or in reaction to "mainstream" values and lifestyles, but that explores the synthesis and integration of gay and lesbian identification with all other aspects of an individual's life.

Characteristics of the stages of the model and terms that we will discuss include *stage equality* and *stage neutrality, multilevelness, private self, public self,* and *psychosocial competence. Stage equality* means that no one stage of coming out is better or worse than another. No individual in a certain stage is superior or inferior to someone at a different level of development, just as being 30 years old is no better or worse per se than being 20.

*Stage neutrality* means that the quality of a person's experience in a given stage will be influenced by the degree of societal homophobia (the environment's neglect of, prejudice toward, and punishment of individuals known to be or suspected of being homosexual); and the extent of internalization of this homophobia in a particular individual in the form of ambivalence and shame about homosexuality. For example, one person may have a relatively tranquil emergence stage while another may experience great confusion, distress, and even despair. What will be different is the amount of societal oppression, both real and imagined, undergone by each person and the consequent amounts of victimization of the two individuals.

*Multilevelness* means that people can have different parts of their lives in different stages—openly gay out of town or with select friends, for example, but closeted with coworkers and family. Stress and change (the loss of a relationship, the move to a new community) may cause the individual to operate at a lower stage until the emotional stress and social isolation is reduced.

*Private self* and *public self* build on the concept of multilevelness to create an individual profile of "outness" that can change over time—disclosure in certain environments and relationships, discretion in others. The *private self* is defined as an intuitive expression of who one is. The *public self* is how one presents oneself to the world at large. The larger the discrepancy between the two selves, the more likely it is that an individual will experience identity confusion and distress and exhibit problems in living. Perhaps the cruelest consequence of homophobia is that we learn to hide our true selves in order to survive and then continue to conceal who we really are in situations and relationships where it may not be necessary.

A primary task facing people with lesbian and gay feelings is to identify and affirm their personal boundaries of sexual self-disclosure and to expand this honest expression into new milieux that are respectful of homosexual identification. The three dimensions of coming out—imagination, knowledge, and experience—are helpful guides to clients or colleagues' current capacity for positive change. What are their hopes and dreams about intimacy and community? What knowledge do they need to support their fantasies? What experiences do they need to test their knowledge? Articulating the three-dimensional nature of coming out can also be an effective antidote to despair. If individuals are too frightened initially to explore their community openly, they can privately build comfort and a sense of group identification by investigating the increasing amount of lesbian and gay literature available. Even more fundamentally, they can begin to identify and clarify their values and aspirations in a safe, informed, respectful, and supportive context.

*Psychosocial competence* is the motivator for positive stage movement. It involves the ability and authority to define and accomplish life tasks. These tasks are seeking normalizing information about homosexuality, identifying community resources, asserting intimacy needs, building personal and professional relationships, and feeling a sense of correctness and effectiveness in pursuit of these developmental goals.

**Coming Out Professionally** Returning to the five-stage model of coming out, we can examine some of the developmental tasks and obstacles to personal and professional competence faced by social workers trying to decide how to integrate their personal self with their professional role.

## Emergence

Most people growing up with gay or lesbian feelings quickly learn that their sexuality is considered by others to be immoral, sick, or criminal. In order to survive and feel a sense of inclusion with family and society, they learn to hide their private selves. They may have a basis for this feeling if they view the situation as dangerous, and rightly so. They probably have experienced or witnessed physical assault, emotional abuse, and psychological coercion directed toward anyone known or suspected to be homosexual. The dilemma that emerges from this early acquired and chronic sense of endangerment can best be expressed as a double bind—"If I interact with others and don't behave appropriately, I'll be noticed (and endangered); if I withdraw, I'll be noticed (and also at risk)." What often results is a situation of compliance in which the individual learns the rules and roles of the heterosexual status quo in order not to be noticed, and thus avoid attack. In social work, that can mean workers with gay and lesbian feelings learn clinical perspectives that interpret their own identity as pathological and then, tragically, pass along this stigma to their homosexual clients as part of keeping a safe cover.

Although major professional organizations no longer regard homosexuality as illness or dysfunction, many practitioners still use outmoded theoretical perspectives based on circular reasoning and bankrupt methodology, and so the legacy of homophobic ignorance remains with us still.[2] Even gay and lesbian workers who reject the illness model of homosexuality may have to work in environments that endorse it. The dangers of homosexual disclosure are very real for these colleagues and, if they feel compliance is their only option, professional identity foreclosure may result.[3] This means giving up hope of ever coming out on the job.

Sadly, these people have created the false equation that endangerment equals capitulation or surrender to the status quo. A powerful alternative to compliance is alliance, which occurs in the next stage.

## Acknowledgment

Acknowledgment of lesbian and gay identity by a worker occurs when one's private self is respected rather than foreclosed. The worker overcomes fear and suspicion to reach out to a peer for identification and support. Danger is still recognized, but is responded to with healthy caution rather than despair, and emerging desires for respectful peer relationships are acknowledged through careful selection of trustworthy confidants. Some workers I know discovered they had a number of possible allies close at hand, while others have traveled across the country to a national conference or phoned long distance to a lesbian/gay task force representative in order to find an understanding and supportive ear.

Overcoming professional isolation can have dramatic effects on workers' self-esteem and assertiveness. Even people who must remain fairly discreet about their sexual identity in their immediate workplace find that peer contact and support have helped them to consider other options for job enhancement. These options include seeking legal counsel to assess workers' rights and job security, openly supporting gay and lesbian clients, encouraging staff education and dialogue on homosexuality, and, if necessary, using new contacts to find employment in a more supportive work environment. Homophobia-related job stress, if not resolvable, becomes much more bearable when shared with others who intimately know the experiences and struggles of being a self-respecting gay or lesbian professional.

Ironically, the most successful acknowledgment experiences can pose unexpected problems. Gay and lesbian social workers whose straight colleagues generally support and welcome their coming out may soon experience a new sort of isolation as the gay or lesbian "expert" on staff. Other interests and competencies may be overlooked. The need for nongay/ nonlesbian staff to work through their own homophobia and to increase knowledge and sensitivity about gay and lesbian clients can be avoided by funneling these cases directly to the identified workers. The worker's sense of mission to the homosexual community may in turn make him or her very susceptible to overcommitment and subsequent burnout.

Workers who have encountered this new "isolation through ascribed expertise" have quickly realized that they are not all things to all homosexual clients. They have countered this overspecialization by encouraging case consultation with nongay colleagues, and by staff development to improve service delivery to the homosexual community on an agencywide basis. Case sharing and providing group therapy with a heterosexual coleader have also proved to be an effective way to disseminate the gay or lesbian worker's knowledge and practice skills with coworkers.

## Workers' Self-Disclosure with Clients

Client-worker relationships are powerful stimuli for workers' identification, clarification, and disclosure of their authentic selves with clients. Continuing exposure to the client's painful struggle to survive in homophobic environments and understand and accept same-sex orientation challenges the worker's sense of professional responsibility. An ethical commitment to provide the best and most comprehensive help may provoke internal conflict with shame, denial, or ambivalence about homosexuality and coming out. As workers seek positive information and community resources for gay and lesbian clients and witness repeated casework successes as a result of being an informed advocate, they may begin to practice what they preach about respect for difference and healthy (discreet, if necessary) coming out.

For the worker who is more comfortably established in a gay or lesbian identity, self-disclosure with lesbian and gay clients can enhance the variables related to successful outcomes in the therapeutic relationship.[4] In clients, these include motivation, confidence in the therapist, and a sense of "voluntariness." For therapists, the qualities of understanding, empathy, warmth, interest, attentiveness, recognition that problems are real rather than imaginary, respect, and being a good listener are enhanced. Particularly helpful is client identification with the therapist's experiences of "being different" and mutual recognition of commonalities in the coming out process for both social worker and client.

## Finding Community

This stage goes beyond individual encounters in a search for a peer group of openly gay and lesbian professionals. A dramatic and inspiring example of how rapidly such a community can develop occurred for me at the 1979 NASW Professional Symposium in San Antonio, Texas. Dozens of lesbian and gay professionals came together, many for the first time, at a workshop on coming out and a later panel presentation of the NASW National Task Force on Lesbian and Gay issues. Some important characteristics of this stage of finding community emerged during the conference:

1. *Strength in numbers.* Although the intellectual realization that 10 percent of our colleagues are gay and lesbian is reassuring, the actual experience of such a sizable peer group is enormously affirming and empowering. As one new friend put it, "Now I really know that I'm not alone anymore";

2. *Public visibility* included many options. Among these were open participation in gay/lesbian-related presentations, lobbying the Delegate Assembly for policy changes and task-force support; dining, shopping, touring, and disco dancing in groups ranging from two to fifty. For people in the earlier stages of coming out, the conference was an invaluable opportunity to practice public expression and enjoyment of their private self, and to experience the beginnings of pride in identity through observation of positive gay and lesbian role models;

3. *A shared history of oppression and liberation.* Gay and lesbian social workers are authorities on the negative consequences of homophobia and can be experts on how to survive and grow in spite of this terrible oppression. The gay and lesbian community at the conference quickly became a "living library" on client and worker victimization and personal and professional survival and growth, sharing together common problems and a wealth of practical solutions.

Finding community is vital to a lesbian or gay social worker's professional identity and development. The NASW Committee on Lesbian and Gay Issues has been organizing state chapters to provide this personal and professional networking and group support to workers and their clients throughout the country. In Minnesota and in other states, the response to such an opportunity to meet and interact with gay and lesbian social workers as well as respectful nongay colleagues has been remarkable. A state task-force-sponsored conference on lesbian and gay life-cycle development drew a hundred participants from around the state, and a recent NASW luncheon seminar on definitions and causes of sexual/affectional orientation broke attendance records for the organization.

What feels most satisfying about the task force is that gay and lesbian social workers now have a visible symbol of the strength and vitality of their professional community. Mere knowledge of the task force has in some cases significantly reduced a worker's sense of isolation and job stress, and active involvement has provided access to positive perspectives on gay client and worker issues, peer empathy and support, and new professional relationships and friendships.

### Building Relationships

Relationship building is a natural extension of finding one's community and can help consolidate the gay and lesbian worker's growing sense of self-respect, pride, and professional competence. Worker empowerment developed in the earlier stages can become more focused and applied to specific areas of need through collaborative endeavors with colleagues, both locally and nationally. This practice manual is a good example of such collaboration and is designed not only to provide relevant knowledge and skills to gay and lesbian workers and clients, but also to connect individuals with similar areas of interest.

Local task forces are developing peer support and supervision groups; sponsoring seminars and conferences; organizing potluck suppers and luncheon meetings; testifying at city councils and state legislatures; consulting with local agencies and practitioners; distributing resource listings and bibliographies; and generally developing visible, solid, and effective working relationships with each other and the community at large. Positive, visible, and assertive gay and lesbian spokespeople are powerful change agents in the struggle to refute the negative myths and stereotypes imposed on our community and to provide public resources for workers and clients who cannot be as open about their identity.

## Self-Definition and Reintegration

This stage is an open-ended one that will last the rest of a worker's career. The first four stages involve exploration of how gay feelings emerge, how they are acknowledged, and how workers find safe people with whom to explore their identity and develop a positive sense of self. Self-definition and reintegration involves looking at every facet of a professional helping role and carefully making decisions about how public one wishes to be with one's gay and lesbian identity. Arrival at this stage means the individual can make these decisions thoughtfully and deliberately and base them on healthy self-interest, pride, and self-respect, rather than on automatic reactions to fear, shame, or a desperate need for approval or acceptance. Since life is a process of change, new situations will provide a continuing challenge to assess carefully the risks and benefits of sharing one's lesbian or gay identity with others.

In summary, coming out in social work and other helping professions can now be seen as a long-term process requiring validation and acceptance of the individual's private self and the development of positive lesbian and gay identity, relationships, and community. Support for a worker's coming out must include respect for individual differences in the extent and pace of their gay or lesbian self-disclosure. Positive movement between stages can be facilitated by obtaining positive information about homosexuality and interacting with openly gay and lesbian peers. With help from colleagues who are further along in the process of professional coming out, individuals can transform isolation and fear into community and hope, and use their past victimizations as a source of compassion and wisdom for the clients and co-workers that they, in turn, can lead out of the closet.

**Notes**

1. John D. Grace, "Coming Out Alive: A Positive Developmental Model of Homosexual Competence, Sixth Biennial Professional Symposium, NASW, San Antonio, Tex., 1979. Mimeographed.

2. Vivienne Cass, "Homosexual Identity Formation: A Theoretical Model," *Journal of Homosexuality*, 4 (Spring 1979), p. 225.

3. John Gonsiorek, "Psychological Adjustment and Homosexuality," *JSAS Catalog of Selected Documents in Psychology* (American Psychological Association), 7, no. 2 (1977), p. 45, MS. 1478.

4. P. Liljestrand, E. Gerlig, and P. A. Saliba, "The Effects of Social Sex-Role Stereotypes and Sexual Orientation on Psychotherapeutic Outcomes," *Journal of Homosexuality*, 3, no. 4, (1978), pp. 361–372.

# Out of the Therapeutic Closet
## Bernice Goodman

**Introduction** The traditional mental health institutions of society, established to deliver services, are archaic. Established from the medical model of pathology, the basic principle of these systems is that people are ill and that professionals will "cure" them. Lesbian/gay people have had to construct many closets in order to survive within hostile and violent systems of "illness" and "treatment." In the following material, the closets of pathology, heterosexism, and the therapist's office are identified. Maintaining these closets and keeping their doors closed have bound therapists in such systems to ineffective interactions and labeling that prevent self-actualization and self-definition of both client and therapist. It is within these oppressive environments that lesbians and gay men have been abused and denied effective and truly professional service for years.

This general oppressive stance has been taken by many therapists in private practice as well as by various institutional personnel—including social workers. This homophobic posture is also true of neo-Freudian, Adlerian, and Gestalt therapists. Even some feminist therapists are guilty of heterosexism. The degree of homophobia will differ but the underlying value system that "homosexuality equals pathology" is still prevalent. The attitude and behavior of the professional ranges from "cure," for example, through "aversion therapy," to a "liberal" position of "having to make the best of it, but, if you have a choice, heterosexuality is better." These positions place lesbian/gay people in great jeopardy, and self-homophobia and oppression are reinforced within the "therapeutic closet," that is, the therapist's office.

**Therapy for Lesbians or Gay Men** In recent years lesbian/gay therapists have been working independently and collectively to establish new models of individual, group, and family therapy. These models are based

140

on values, attitudes, and knowledge outlined in other sections of this manual. The essence of this approach is beautifully stated in June Jordan's poem:

### A Short Note to My Very Critical and Well-Beloved Friends and Comrades

First they said I was too light
Then they said I was too dark
Then they said I was too different
Then they said I was too much the same
Then they said I was too young
Then they said I was too old
Then they said I was too interracial
Then they said I was too much a nationalist
Then they said I was too silly
Then they said I was too angry
Then they said I was too idealistic
Then they said I was too confusing altogether:
Make up your mind! They said. Are you militant
or sweet? Are you vegetarian or meat? Are you
    straight
or are you gay?
And I said, Hey! It's not about *my* mind.[1]

In order to begin to correct this appalling situation, individually and collectively, lesbian/feminist and gay male therapists as well as empathetic, knowledgable nongay professionals are establishing other patterns of delivering service to those in need.

As one way to break this pattern, I would suggest a threefold approach: (1) administrators in mental health and related systems should encourage greater self-examination by staff relative to homophobia; (2) therapists should be alert to the need for ever-increased sensitivity and knowledge related to issues of concern to lesbians and gay males; (3) helping professionals should be willing to look at their own attitudes in the engagement process of therapy and involve clients in assuring that there is a "fit" between therapist and client that will maximize self-actualization. These goals can be monitored by administration, therapists, *and* clients by giving attention to the following questions (and the answers that are given!).

1. What firsthand knowledge does the therapist have about the lesbian and gay culture? How many lesbian/gay clients has she or he helped? How long has the therapist been working with lesbian/gay clients?

2. How much understanding and knowledge does the therapist have about racism, sexism, and homophobia in our society?

3. Is the therapist committed to a concept of "difference" rather than "sameness"?[2]

4. Does this therapist understand that institutional homophobia is an illness and that lesbian/gay people are victims of the social illness?

5. Can this therapist articulate the differences between real societal oppressions and appropriate behavior responses related to this, from real intrapsychic difficulties that a lesbian/gay person may be experiencing?

6. Can this therapist distinguish between programmed negative definitions of self as a woman and internal, positive, organic psychic feelings of self as woman?

7. Can this therapist help men to deal with their feelings about differing from societally defined and imposed images of being a "real man"? Is this therapist able to raise questions within the gay male community in terms of the "economically reinforced macho image" versus an attitude of "not acknowledging our oppression as men"?

8. Is this therapist free to challenge self-oppressive attitudes that the client holds about self and to support new self-creative and expansive feelings?

9. How, and in what way, does this therapist participate in the lesbian and gay community?

10. Is this therapist willing to engage with clients in community activities outside of the therapy interaction? Can the therapist understand the qualities that are different in these two types of interactions?[3]

11. Do client and therapist like each other? Does the therapist generate a feeling of trust and safety and seem

secure and free and happy to participate as a therapist in the interactional process of therapy?

12. How willing is the therapist and/or agency to negotiate terms and means of payment (for example, sliding scale, barter, work exchange, and so forth) or do they give the impression that the payment is more important than the client?

There are, of course, great variations in culture, ethnicity, and values among lesbians and gay men. Because of this, each lesbian/gay client should be helped to organize a checklist of what is important in the therapeutic process and the client-therapist relationship.

Other guidelines for agency practices would include:

1. Does the waiting room have lesbian/gay magazines and literature?

2. Does written material describing agency services include lesbian/gay people and their needs?

3. How many staff meetings are devoted to lesbian/gay issues, as well as to other alternate lifestyles?

4. How many open lesbian/gay professionals/workers are on the staff of the agency?

5. Does the agency encourage clients to feel free to ask for a therapist who is knowledgable about lesbian/gay culture and who has been retrained to recognize homophobic attitudes, values, and practices?

The ultimate goal of therapy is for each of us to become our own authority on, and in charge of, our individual and community life. This occurs when our feelings of internal and inherent harmony are freed.

This liberation is essential to all human existence. Lesbian/gay people have insisted on this quality of life in their individual and collective efforts in all areas of social interaction. This must include therapeutic interactions, and reeducated social workers can assist in this process of empowerment and rejection of oppression.

The self-actualization of lesbian and gay clients, or participants in therapy, demands the end of the therapeutic closet.

**Notes**     1. June Jordan, *Passion: New Poems, 1977–1980* (Boston: Beacon Press, 1980), p. 78. Copyright © 1980 by June Jordan. Reprinted by permission of Beacon Press.

2. The difference model celebrates the uniqueness of each individual. Although the significance of our personal uniqueness has frequently been overlooked, the evidence of difference is intrinsic to each one of us. Witness the biological fact that no two people, among the millions who inhabit this earth, have the same fingerprints and that the intrapsychic forces of our personality that distinguish us from one another are uniquely different.

The concept of sameness has come to represent and to color much of modern experience. It encourages us to conform at any cost, to fit into the mold, to allow ourselves to be controlled, to hate people different in color, ethnicity, or sex. Our existence is threatened by our failure to acknowledge and challenge the culture of sameness (Bernice Goodman, *The Lesbian: A Celebration of Difference* [New York: Out & Out Books, 1977], pp. 27–29).

3. Because of the lack of family support of gay people, therapists should try when possible to support their clients outside the therapy sessions. This can take the form of attending key family functions and performances, participating together in meetings and conferences, and, in some instances, creating friendships. These nontraditional frontiers can create some therapeutic problems, but the advantages far outweigh the problems (Goodman, *The Lesbian,* p. 36).

# A Prototype for a Comprehensive Continuing Education Program on Gay and Lesbian Issues
## Travis L. Peterson

On November 15, 1980, Houston's first major continuing education program on gay/lesbian issues was conducted for mental health professionals. "Omnibus: Lesbian and Gay Issues in Mental Health Practice" was sponsored by the University of Houston Graduate School of Social Work and Continuing Education Center, the Association for Lesbian and Gay Mental Health, the Montrose Counseling Center, and the Task Force on Lesbian and Gay Issues of the Texas Chapter of the National Association of Social Workers. The following workshops, as presented at Houston, are suggested for inclusion in similar programs elsewhere:

"The Negative Effects of Homophobia" (with a nationally renowned speaker).

**Major Address**

1. "Alcoholism Treatment with the Homosexual Population." Alcoholism is a serious problem within the lesbian/gay community and is exacerbated by pressure from society. Professional and indigenous perspectives regarding treatment will be presented.

**Workshop Topics**

2. "Everything You've Always Wanted to Know about Being Lesbian/Gay But Were Afraid to Ask." The panel members and service consumers will present perspectives on being lesbian/gay. Your questions and concerns will receive understanding and nonjudgmental responses.

3. "Health Care Issues in Lesbian/Gay Subcultures." Health care needs in the lesbian and gay communities are unique.

This panel of health care professionals will address these needs, as well as nuances in the relationships between medical professionals and patients.

4. "Psychological Functioning of the Lesbian/Gay Person." Homosexually oriented persons are repeatedly given the message by society that they must be something different than what they feel inside. This hampers their ability to trust not only their genuine, internal instincts, but makes it difficult for them to trust others, including the mental health professional. This panel will examine some of these issues and their very real implications for the practice of social work.

5. "The Role of Religion in Mental Health/Illness of the Homosexually Oriented." The traditional Judeo-Christian attitude toward sexual activities will be explored to establish its impact on lesbians and gays and its effect with regard to guilt, religious communal expression, and a sense of the sacred. Discussion of alternative religious groups will help to provide information about the current services available to the gay community.

6. "Alternatives to Treatment: Does Every Homosexual Need Therapy?" This session will educate the mental health professional as to common personality development issues and stages in the "coming out" process of the homosexual person. Positive alternatives for both men and women will be presented.

7. "The Lesbian/Gay Couple in Treatment: Special Nuances." This workshop will focus on the differences and similarities between homosexual and heterosexual couples. Lesbian and gay male coupling will also be differentiated. Special emphasis will be placed on intervention techniques.

8. "Lesbian/Gay Communities—Going to the Source for Resources." Gay and lesbian resources are available for peer support, professional interaction, and social development in accepting environments. Know and use your community resources.

9. "Stress in the Family of the Homosexual Person." Panelists will explore the issues around working with families of lesbians/gays in crisis or in a therapeutic setting. They will address the grief, shock, and pain experienced by the families

of gay persons or lesbian women, and the necessity of working through these feelings.

10. "The Gay/Lesbian Adolescent-at-Large in the Community: What Can Be Done?" Teenagers, aware or afraid of attraction to the same sex, experience more difficulty securing services than do adults. Their status as minors influences many professionals to shy away. Who will serve as advocates? What can the professional community do to influence more positive alternatives?

# Some Guidance and Advice for a Continuing Education Session on Gay and Lesbian Issues
## Margaret Nichols and Michael Shernoff

**P**articipants—Nongay social service professionals representing a broad range of disciplines, agency affiliations, and job functions. These will probably include well-meaning professionals who, out of ignorance or unconscious assimilation of society's homophobic values, unknowingly and unwillingly damage their gay/lesbian clients.

*Trainers*—An "out" lesbian and gay professional team. It is important that the team members have resolved enough of their own anger that they are able to be personally revealing and nonantagonistic with a nongay audience. (See chapter by John Grace in this manual.)

*Political/Philosophical Perspective*—Should gays/lesbians utilize the services of a nongay professional? Can straight professionals provide sensitive, nonhomophobic services to gay and lesbian clients? Realistically, gays and lesbians will in many, if not most, cases have to utilize nongay/nonlesbian professionals or closeted gays and lesbians to meet their counseling and other social service needs. Training and sensitization of nongay/nonlesbian counselors and human service workers are therefore critical if the lesbian/gay community is to be helped.

**Session Plan and Suggestions (Two-to-three-hour sessions)**

### What

1. Spend time to guide, cajole, and encourage participants to explore and reveal their homophobic attitudes.

This chapter was adapted by Hilda Hidalgo from Margaret Nichols and Michael Shernoff, "Training Mental Health Professionals to Work with Lesbians and Gay Men," unpublished manuscript, Highland Park, N.J., 1982.

2. Participants must never feel that the workshop is an adversarial procedure.

3. Participants must feel permitted to express attitudes, feelings, and beliefs that their liberal consciences tell them are "bad," "prejudiced," "not nice," or politically incorrect.

4. Define concepts such as *heterosexism* and *homophobia*.

5. Discuss how these phenomena oppress lesbian and gay men in the social service settings.

6. Guide participants through one or two sensitivity exercises.

7. Provide some factual data about gay and lesbian lifestyles.

8. Present the concept of sexual/affectional orientation.

9. Discuss the onset of sexual feelings before or during early adolescence (dispel the assumption that, if the sexual orientation is homosexual, it is malleable and subject to change).

10. Stress the importance of developing a positive gay/lesbian identity for the client and the struggle involved in this process.

    a. Discuss the importance of openness to gays and lesbians (how heterosexuals "flaunt" their heterosexuality).

    b. Discuss the risks involved in coming out.

    c. Provide information about local support groups for gays and lesbians.

11. Tailor your presentation to the particular population served by the participants as determined by agency and function.

### How

1. Establish a tone and atmosphere in which participants feel free to "join with" trainers. Trainers should

    a. Reveal something of their personal histories, concentrating on the stages of their own confusion and fear about homosexuality.

    b. Tell participants that trainers perceive them as caring, empathetic individuals who want to help their lesbian/gay clients, that everyone inevitably acquires misinformed, prejudiced attitudes toward homosexuality through growing up in a homophobic society.

Continuing Education: Guidance    **149**

c. Share your personal struggle to dispel homophobia.

d. Assure participants that nothing they say will offend the trainer or be taken personally.

2. Give examples—consult and gather material from other sections of this resource manual; for example, in an intake interview, the question, Are you married or single?, is an innocent question that is based on heterosexism.

3. Select some examples from this section of the resource manual and from the Appendixes.

4. Share material from the section References by Content Area in this resource manual.

5. Use the Kinsey continuum of sexual orientation; Masters and Johnson's findings regarding heterosexual fantasies among homosexuals and homosexual fantasies among heterosexuals; and John Money's concepts of "limerance" (refers to the "infatuation stage" of falling in love).[1]

6. Ask participants to think back to their earliest childhood/ adolescent attractions—when they realized they were heterosexual—to sensitize them to just how clear-cut and defined the adolescent sexual orientation often is.

7. Make analogies between the social situations of gays and lesbians and that of other groups in similar situations: blacks trying to "pass"; the self-hate (internalization of racism) of blacks; the internalization of homophobia by lesbians and gays; Jews "passing as gentiles" in an anti-Semitic society; and so on.

a. Use the Heterosexual Questionnaire in Appendix G to this resource manual.

b. Use the chapter on coming out by John Grace and those chapters on legal issues by Kathleen Mayer and Fern Schwaber.

c. Give name, address, phone number of local gay/lesbian groups, bars, social clubs, and so on.

8. Include in your examples role-playing situations and sensitivity exercises related to those situations most frequently encountered in the client population served by the participants.

1. Alfred C. Kinsey, Wardell B. Pomeroy, and Clyde E. **Note**
Martin, *Sexual Behavior in the Human Male* (Philadelphia: W.
B. Saunders Co., 1948); William H. Masters and Virginia
Johnson, *Homosexuality in Perspective* (Boston: Little, Brown
& Co., 1979); and John Money, *Love and Love Sickness: The
Science of Sex, Gender, Difference, and Pair Bonding* (Baltimore,
Md.: Johns Hopkins University Press, 1980).

# Two-Hour In-Service Training Session on Homophobia
## A. Elfin Moses and Robert O. Hawkins, Jr.

**General Guidelines**  The in-service training described here consists of three parts: definition of terms, assessment of participants' own homophobic attitudes, and discussion of the impact of homophobia on social workers and their clients. We provide an outline for each part as well as some suggestions for making the in-service training session maximally effective.

The material presented is intended primarily as a suggestive framework that will allow others to use their own creativity, incorporate their own ideas, and add new information and techniques as these become available. In using this outline ourselves, we find that differences among and within various groups may dictate changes in the way we plan a particular session. Indeed, we may make changes during the course of an in-service training session as participants raise questions or ask for things not provided for in the outline. We find that these guidelines work best when we are flexible in using them.

**Definitions**  The following definitions should either be distributed to participants or written on a blackboard:

1. Homosexual: A person who engages in sexual activity with someone of the same gender.

2. Homoerotic: Having a preference for affectional and physical relationships with someone of the same gender identity; specifically, a lesbian woman or a gay man.

3. Gender: Biological maleness or femaleness. May differ from gender identity.

4. Gender identity: Internalization of gender; belief that one is male or female. May differ from gender.

152

5. Gender role behavior: Overt behaviors associated with a particular gender within a given culture.

6. Homophobia: An unrealistic fear of or generalized negative attitude toward homoerotic people; fear of homosexuality. Homophobia may be experienced and expressed by lesbians and gay men as well as by nongays.

### Suggestions (Using Definitions)

Time can profitably be spent discussing the difference between the concepts of "homosexual" and "homoerotic." It is particularly important to note that not everyone who engages in sexual behavior with someone of the same gender is homoerotic nor is everyone who engages in sexual behavior with someone of the opposite gender heteroerotic.

It is also a good idea to discuss the implications of various labels such as "lesbian," "gay," and "homosexual." Leaders of the in-service training may also want to use terms like "nongay" and "nonlesbian" and contrast the use of these terms with the terms "heterosexual" and "straight." Boswell and Moses and Hawkins discuss these issues, and Jay and Young report preferences of those in their sample for various terms, so it might be worthwhile to refer to these sources prior to the inservice.[1]

Another important, and sometimes difficult, idea to get across is that gay men and lesbian women are not suffering from a gender dysfunction or from gender identity confusion. Both gay men and lesbian women know which gender they belong to and demonstrate behavior patterns typical of nongay individuals of their gender. The major difference between nongays and gays is in sexual and affectional preference.

The following questions are often most effectively presented in a questionnaire format so that participants have a chance to answer them privately before a group discussion ensues. **Assessment of Personal Homophobia**

1. Do you stop yourself from doing or saying certain things because someone might think you're gay or lesbian? If yes, what kinds of things?

2. Do you ever intentionally do or say things so that

people will think you're nongay? If yes, what kinds of things?

3. Do you believe that gays or lesbians can influence others to become homoerotic? Do you think someone could influence you to change your sexual and affectional preference?

4. If you are a parent, how would you (or do you) feel about having a lesbian daughter or gay son?

5. How do you think you would feel if you discovered that one of your parents or parent figures, or a brother or sister, were gay or lesbian?

6. Are there any jobs, positions, or professions that you think lesbians and gays should be barred from holding or entering? If yes, why so?

7. Would you go to a physician whom you knew or believed to be gay or lesbian if that person were of a different gender from you? If that person were of the same gender as you? If not, why not?

8. If someone you care about were to say to you, "I think I'm gay," would you suggest that the person see a therapist?

9. Have you ever been to a gay or lesbian bar, social club, party, or march? If not, why not?

10. Would you wear a button that says, "How dare you assume that I'm heterosexual"? If not, why not?

11. Can you think of three positive aspects of a gay or lesbian lifestyle? Can you think of three negative aspects of a nongay lifestyle?

12. Have you ever laughed at a "queer" joke?

## Suggestions (Using Questions)

Be sure that people have plenty of time to answer the questions before you discuss them. If you ask the questions aloud, you may want to suggest that people jot down their answers on a sheet of paper. This will give people time to think for a minute or two about each item.

Begin the discussion by commenting that everyone in the room is probably homophobic to some extent, just as we are almost all racist and sexist to some extent. Holding stereotypes is nothing to be ashamed of, but rather is a human characteristic. It is not helpful, however, if we hold inaccurate beliefs or have feelings about groups of people based on misinformation, fear, or ignorance. It is up to each individual to examine her or his own beliefs and to determine to what extent these may be incorrect and may be harmful to others.

The leader or trainer should know possible answers to each of the questions and should be able to provide accurate information, as well as to discuss how certain answers may indicate homophobia. If the group of people present do not provide any homophobic responses, which is not an uncommon occurrence particularly among "enlightened" social workers, the leader should suggest some.

If no participants are openly gay or lesbian, the leader can also remind everyone that because approximately one out of seven people is homoerotic, if there are seven or more people in the room, at least one person is probably gay or lesbian. It is often instructive to ask how participants think a lesbian or gay person might answer the questions and how she or he might feel hearing the responses of nongay participants.

1. Personal homophobia on the part of social workers can result in inadequate, improper, and harmful services to gay and lesbian clients and those related to or dependent on them. Discuss personal attitudes and their importance in worker-client, worker-worker, and worker-community interactions. Professionalism dictates being aware of one's own attitudes and referring clients when these attitudes may get in the way of provision of high-quality services.

**Impact of Homophobia on Social Workers and Their Clients**

2. Societal homophobia leads to unequal treatment and stigmatization of lesbian and gay clients. It may also lead to restriction of behavior so that individuals of both genders may not perform the full range of behaviors of which they are capable. For example, in a homophobic society, so-called "feminine" behaviors and feelings are punished in boys and men, whereas so-called "masculine" behaviors are punished in girls and women.

3. Homophobia in agencies prevents social workers from

accomplishing their goals, providing complete services, and so forth. Homophobia in agencies can be discussed in the context of agencies such as hospitals, prisons, community mental health centers, child and family service agencies, agencies serving those who are hearing or visually impaired, services for the aging, and so forth. Particular attention can be given to AIDS patients and their significant others, lesbian and gay alcoholics, lesbian and gay couples, and lesbian and gay parents and their children.

### Suggestions to Combat Homophobia

It is important in each area not only to identify problems but to discuss possible solutions and courses of action. It is easy and tempting in these kinds of sessions to spend a lot of time on "war stories." Although personal experiences are beneficial in that they provide real-life examples and engage participants emotionally, the process should not stop there. How can one combat homophobia in oneself, in society, in one's agency? Be prepared to provide participants with specific, simple, and realistic suggestions.

Personal homophobia is best combated in two ways. First, gather information through reading, talking to people, and listening to music created by gays. (There is an especially large collection of music for women, written and performed by lesbians.) Suggestions for such material are provided in the References by Content Area. Second, get to know some lesbian women and gay men personally. Research has shown that the best way to combat stereotypes is to have contact with the people about whom one holds such stereotypes.

Societal homophobia is obviously more difficult to combat, but certainly the more individuals become informed the better off we are. Presentations to church groups, schools, agency personnel, and the like are all possibilities.

Homophobia in agencies is probably the hardest to combat because those who would do so must risk being labeled. Any discussion of homophobia should also include discussion of the risks and realities of living in a homophobic society. Some relatively nonthreatening ways to combat homophobia in agencies are to respond assertively to homophobic jokes and comments, to provide reading materials, to educate, and to equate nonhomophobic attitudes with other desirable qualities such as intelligence, compassion, sensitivity, competence, open-mindedness, and general all-around wonderfulness.

1. John Boswell, *Christianity, Social Tolerance, and Homosex-* **Note** *uality: Gay People in Western Europe from the Beginning of the Christian Era to the Fourteenth Century* (Chicago: University of Chicago Press, 1980); A. Elfin Moses and Robert O. Hawkins, *Counseling Lesbian Women and Gay Men: A Life-Issues Approach* (St. Louis, Mo.: C. V. Mosby Co., 1982); and Karla Jay and Allen Young, *The Gay Report* (New York: Summit Books, 1979).

# APPENDIXES

# Appendix A

The NASW Code of Ethics, adopted in 1979 by the NASW **NASW Code** Delegate Assembly, states: "The social worker *should not prac-* **of Ethics** *tice, condone, facilitate or collaborate with any form of discrimination on the basis of* race, color, sex, *sexual orientation,* age, religion, national origin, *marital status,* political belief, mental or physical handicap, or any other *preference* or *personal characteristic,* condition or *status*."[1] (Italics added to the words of the anti-discriminatory statement that relate directly to the lesbian and gay lifestyles.)

---

[1] "Code of Ethics of the National Association of Social Workers," NASW Policy Statements 1 (Silver Spring, Md.: NASW, July 1, 1980), p. 4.

# Appendix B

**NASW Public Social Policy Statement on Gay Issues** The National Association of Social Workers realizes that homosexuality has existed under varying circumstances, throughout recorded history and in most cultures. A substantial number of women and men in American society are identified with a lifestyle that includes homosexual behavior. Homosexuality may properly be considered a preference, orientation, or propensity for certain kinds of lifestyles. Millions of men and women, whose sexual orientation includes homosexuality, are subject to severe social, psychological, economic, and legal discrimination because of their sexual orientation.

NASW views discrimination and prejudice directed against any minority as inimical to the mental health not only of the affected minority, but of the society as a whole. The Association deplores and will work to combat archaic laws, discriminatory employment practices, and other forms of discrimination which serve to impose something less than equal status upon the homosexually-oriented members of the human family. It is the objective of the social work profession not only to bring health and welfare services closer to people, but also to help alter the unequal policies and practices of health and welfare institutions.

NASW affirms the right of all persons to define and express their own sexuality. In choosing their own lifestyle, all persons are to be encouraged to develop their individual potential to the fullest extent possible as long as they do not impinge upon the rights of others.

---

Adopted by the NASW Delegate Assembly, Portland, Oreg., 1977.

Acquired Immune Deficiency Syndrome (AIDS) presents a public health crisis to the nation. Much can be done by social workers and other helping professionals to foster knowledge, heighten the awareness of and response to it by various institutions, marshall social resources, and otherwise mediate and assist those individuals and their loved ones who are affected by AIDS. Because of the complex biopsychosocial issues presented by AIDS, social workers, with their special knowledge, skills and sensitivity, are uniquely capable of responding to this crisis by pursuing action in each of the following areas: (1) research, (2) public education and dissemination of information, (3) psychological and social supports, (4) community development, (5) civil rights, and (6) professional accountability.

**NASW Public Social Policy Statement on AIDS**

---

Excerpt from "Acquired Immune Deficiency Syndrome," adopted by the NASW Delegate Assembly, Washington, D.C., 1984.

# Appendix C

**Goals of the NASW National Task Force on Lesbian and Gay Issues (1979–82)**

1. To help create a professional environment that is conducive to professional and personal growth of gay social workers.

2. To attain quality of social work services for lesbian and gay male clients.

3. To achieve full recognition within NASW of the reality of the minority status of lesbians and gay men.

4. To accomplish the review of all existing structures, publications, and policies of NASW to assure they reflect the NASW policy statement on gay issues.

5. To facilitate the formation of lesbian and gay issues task forces and committees in all chapters.

6. To organize and develop a nationwide network of gay male and lesbian social workers who will serve as regional resource persons for consultation, in-service education, and research of local needs and problems relative to the NASW policy statement on gay issues.

7. To encourage lesbian and gay male social workers and students to "come out of their closets" professionally and work toward the full implementation of the NASW policy statement on gay issues. Further, to utilize the available resources of NASW, including the role of advocacy, in the pursuit of justice in the event that discrimination occurs.

8. To assure that NASW, through its existing structures, responds to legislation and media presentations that affect the health and welfare of gay male and lesbian clients and social workers.

9. To create and participate in coalitions with any organizations and groups on common issues, with particular emphasis on the task force created by the Council on Social Work Education.*

---

*CSWE's task force is now called the Commission on Gay/Lesbian Issues in Social Work Education.

The purpose of the National Committee on Lesbian and Gay Issues is to enable NASW to further the cause of social justice by promoting and defending the rights of persons suffering injustices and oppression because of their homosexual orientation.

**Purpose and History of the NASW National Committee on Lesbian and Gay Issues (1982–present)**

NASW's sensitivity to the need for professional recognition and support for lesbian/gay social workers and lesbian/gay clients was heightened in the early 1970's principally through the efforts of a small group of very visible and committed social workers. These individuals prepared and presented workshops and position papers on sexual orientation issues and social work practice at NASW's symposia and Delegate Assemblies. A small group of social workers began working with NASW leadership on an informal basis to assess ways in which the Association could be more responsive to its gay members and to develop strategies for obtaining NASW's inclusion of "sexual orientation" in its anti-discrimination policies on social agencies' personnel practices and its union contract with national office staff.

In 1977, the NASW Delegate Assembly adopted the Public Policy Statement on Gay Issues. In 1979, the NASW Task Force on Lesbian and Gay Issues was appointed. Task Force members worked diligently to promote the visibility of lesbian and gay concerns within the Association, nationally and in chapters throughout the country. In 1982, the NASW National Board of Directors created the National Committee on Lesbian and Gay Issues as a standing unit of the Association.

**CSWE Action**   The action taken by the Board of Directors of the Council on Social Work Education (CSWE) is contained in the following paragraph excerpted from the curriculum policy statement:

> The curriculum must provide content on ethnic minorities of color and women. It should include content on other special population groups relevant to the program's mission or location and, in particular, groups that have been consistently affected by social, economic and legal bias or oppression. Such groups include, but are not limited to, those distinguished by age, religion, disablement, *sexual orientation* and culture. [Italics added.][1]

CSWE's Baccalaureate Evaluative Standard 11 and MSW Evaluation Standard 12 address the same issue:

> Every aspect of the program's organization and implementation shall be conducted without discrimination on the basis of race, color, gender, age, creed, ethnic or national origin, handicap, or political or *sexual orientation.* [Italics added.][2]

---

[1] "Curriculum Policy for the Master's Degree and Baccalaureate Degree Programs In Social Work Education" (New York: Council on Social Work Education, 1982), unpaginated.

[2] Commission on Accreditation, *Handbook of Accreditation Standards and Procedures* (New York: Council on Social Work Education, July 1984), Sec. 1·5, Sec. 2·5.

# Appendix D

In 1981, Nancy Humphreys (president of NASW in 1979–81) stated:

> Knowledge of and sensitivity to gay and lesbian issues are a necessary part of the social worker's practice repertoire for at least three good reasons. First, gays and lesbians who receive social services from social workers are becoming an increasingly larger constituent group of the profession. Second, many social workers are gay or lesbian, some of whom are out of the closet, but quite a few of whom still choose to hide themselves in order to evade the stigma society attaches to the gay person. Third, and perhaps most importantly, gay and lesbian people represent an oppressed population, the protection of whose rights, as those of all oppressed populations, should be of primary concern to the profession of social work.[1]

Humphreys recalled that on other occasions social workers had failed to face and fight discrimination and oppression, and that they had regretted it later. Humphreys recognized the link among homophobia, racism, sexism, and ageism—all resulting from institutionalized socialization processes "which seek to promote conformity and limit difference."[2] She exhorted social workers "to be aware of and prepare to vigorously oppose efforts to oppress and suppress differences, not only the more overt and crude efforts, but those more subtle and often more difficult to detect and deal with."[3]

Mary Ann Quaranta (president of NASW in 1981–83), in a position statement submitted to the National Task Force on Lesbian and Gay Issues in July 1979, had indicated her strong support of the NASW policy statement on gay and lesbian issues:

---

[1] Nancy Humphreys, "From the President," *NASW News,* 26 (May 1981), p. 2.
[2] Ibid.
[3] Ibid.

As an individual and as a social worker, I endorse the NASW resolution on Gay Issues. The social work profession has as its heritage a commitment to work toward the eradication of discrimination in any form. As professionals, we are committed to a principle which holds that the individual has the right to exercise choice in the manner in which one lives and in one's lifestyle. Over the years, social workers have advocated for the rights of children, ethnic and racial minorities, women and countless others and today, we must advocate on behalf of gay and lesbian people as part of this tradition of advocacy.

I support the policy statement and the recommended implementation of the NASW statement. I would see three primary areas for our immediate attention. First, we need to sensitize the social work profession by providing information and direction related to Gay Issues. I would look to the National Task Force as a resource in this area to provide the members of our profession the opportunity to develop their personal awareness and to incorporate this into their practice. Secondly, NASW itself must be a model and reflect our commitment to gay social workers by supporting the National Task Force and moving toward implementation of the resolution. Lastly, our schools of social work carry a primary responsibility to incorporate gay issues into both knowledge-based courses and practice courses to enable social workers in training to integrate gay issues into their own professional practice.

# Appendix E

1. *Brief Program Description:* (Focus and goals, content, and sensitizing experiences about homosexual people/homosexual social work professionals)

2. *Program Format and Schedule:* (Workshop, institute, forum, etc. —time concentration, commuter or residential, etc., total number of hours/days, preferred month[s] of year)

3. *Proposal Location(s):*

4. *Participants:* (Target numbers, background, experience, etc.)

5. *Person(s) Responsible for Planning:*

6. *Lead Time Required for Planning:*

7. *Speakers/Other Resource Persons:*

8. *Proposed Budget—Income and Expenses:*

9. *Assistance Required from Professional Development Committee:* (Technical support in planning, budgeting, publicizing, evaluation, etc.)

**Professional Development Program Proposal**

---

Proposal outline by Carol Tully.

I. PARTICIPANTS:

A. Who is attending and how many? (Get this information from preregistration and registration forms.)

B. What are their needs concerning gay and lesbian issues?

II. FOCUS FOR LEARNING ACTIVITIES: (Check areas of importance to your staff and answer the appropriate questions.)

| | | |
|---|---|---|
| | Getting information: | What kinds of information? |
| | Identifying or dealing with feelings and attitudes: | What kinds of feelings and attitudes? |
| | Identifying and solving problems: | What kinds of problems? |
| | Practicing skills: | Which skills? |
| | Other: | Explain. |

## III. GOALS FOR LEARNING ACTIVITIES:

| Participant's Goals | Facilitator's Methodology |
|---|---|
| 1. | 1. |
| 2. | 2. |
| 3. | 3. |
| 4. | 4. |

## IV. MATERIALS (OR PORTIONS OF MATERIALS) TO BE USED:

| Item | Portion | Why | Approximate Time |
|---|---|---|---|
| | | | |
| | | | |
| | | | |
| | | | |

## V. NUMBER OF SESSIONS _____.
## LENGTH OF TIME FOR EACH SESSION _____.

**Organizational Membership Questionnaire**

*Sample questionnaire useful in soliciting membership input on content for in-service training. It is important that NASW chapter stationery be used in all official announcements and correspondence, because it gives professional legitimacy to the task force or groups organizing the event.*

The Gay Issues Committee and the Professional Development Committee of State Chapter, NASW, are planning a one-day educational institute related to homosexuality to be held early in 1986 in Capital City. To assure that the institute meets your professional needs, we would appreciate your completing the following brief "needs assessment" questionnaire and mailing it back to us within ten days after receipt. Your response will let the Gay Issues Committee know your needs and enable them to provide you with meaningful information.

1. Please consider the following list of possible topic areas in light of *your* needs as a professional social worker and select three you would like to see covered in an institute.

   (Prioritize: 1—high need; 2—moderate need; 3—need)

   \_\_\_\_ Working with homosexual clients

   \_\_\_\_ Resources for homosexuals within the community

   \_\_\_\_ Homosexual professionals in social work

   \_\_\_\_ Working with the gay alcoholic

   \_\_\_\_ Information on homosexual lifestyles and social behaviors

   \_\_\_\_ Homophobia: Causes and Cures

   \_\_\_\_ Legal issues about homosexuality

   \_\_\_\_ The older homosexual

   \_\_\_\_ Services to homosexual juveniles

   \_\_\_\_ Homosexual mothers and juveniles

   \_\_\_\_ Other (Please specify) _____

   _____

2. Please consider the following list of possible topic areas in light of the needs of your agency, your staff, your geographical locale and prioritize the top three.

(Prioritize: 1—high need; 2—moderate need; 3—need)

_____ Working with homosexual clients

_____ Resources for homosexuals within the community

_____ Homosexual professionals in social work

_____ Information on homosexual lifestyles and sexual behaviors

_____ Homophobia: Causes and Cures

_____ Legal issues about homosexuality

_____ The older homosexual

_____ Services to homosexual juveniles

_____ Homosexual mothers and fathers

_____ Other (Please specify) _____

_____

3. Would you be interested in attending a one-day institute that addressed the needs you noted?

_____ Yes

_____ No

_____ Not sure

Your help with this is appreciated by the new Chapter Committee. If you are interested in joining or helping this Committee (all folks welcome) contact:

PLEASE RETURN THIS QUESTIONNAIRE WITHIN TEN DAYS TO:

**Personal Learning Objectives**

*This form could be useful if distributed at the end of a training session for participants to commit themselves to continuing their personal growth and learning in relation to lesbian and gay issues.*

| Objectives for learning, change, or improvement | Timeline for accomplishing | First steps in meeting chosen objectives |
|---|---|---|
| 1. In assessing my values and attitudes about gay- or lesbian-identified people, I will | | |
| 2. In finding and using relevant resources in these areas for my clinical practice or school of social work, I will | | |
| 3. In order to increase my personal and professional comfort and skill levels with these issues, I will | | |
| 4. In supporting the implementation of programs for professionals and community concerning affectional preference issues, I will | | |
| 5. In order to put homosexuality back into the context of family, I will | | |
| 6. Others... | | |

# Appendix F

*Word Is Out* is a film available in 1- or 2½-hour versions **Sample Program** that will provoke feelings and discussion from the audience. **Meeting** Plan to provide time for discussion afterward. Viewing could be planned in conjunction with a social get-together and is a good "starter activity" for newly formed committees on gay and lesbian issues. The film is available from: New Yorker Films, 16 W. 61st St., New York, N.Y. 10023 (for anyone) and Arizona Chapter of NASW, Committee on Lesbian and Gay Issues, 6722 N. 23rd Place, Phoenix, Ariz. 85016, (602) 956-5848 (for NASW chapters only).

*Word Is Out* is a fascinating feature-length documentary that provides a candid glimpse into the lives of twenty-six homosexual men and women. The participants in the film discuss their childhoods, families, love relationships, and the often-painful road to self-acceptance, creating a remarkably coherent chronicle of what it is like to grow up "different" in the United States. This film presentation offers social workers a base for understanding a variety of homosexual life experiences.

# Appendix G

*This Heterosexual Questionnaire reverses the questions that are very often asked of gays and lesbians by straight people. By having to answer this type of question, the heterosexual person will get some intellectual and emotional insight into how oppressive and discriminatory a "straight" frame of reference can be to lesbians and gays.*

1. What do you think caused your heterosexuality?

2. When and how did you first decide you were a heterosexual?

3. Is it possible that your heterosexuality is just a phase you may grow out of?

4. Is it possible that your heterosexuality stems from a neurotic fear of others of the same sex?

5. If you've never slept with a person of the same sex, is it possible that all you need is a good gay lover?

6. To whom have you disclosed your heterosexual tendencies?

7. Why do you heterosexuals feel compelled to seduce others into your lifestyle?

8. Why do you insist on flaunting your heterosexuality? Can't you just be what you are and keep it quiet?

9. Would you want your children to be heterosexual, knowing the problem they'd face?

10. A disproportionate majority of child molesters are heterosexuals. Do you consider it safe to expose your children to heterosexual teachers?

11. Even with all the societal support marriage receives, the divorce rate is spiraling. Why are there so few stable relationships among heterosexuals?

12. Why do heterosexuals place so much emphasis on sex?

13. Considering the menace of overpopulation, how could the human race survive if everyone were heterosexual like you?

---

Questionnaire by Martin Rochlin.

14. Could you trust a heterosexual therapist to be objective? Don't you fear that the therapist might be inclined to influence you in the direction of his or her own leanings?

15. How can you become a whole person if you limit yourself to compulsive, exclusive heterosexuality and fail to develop your natural, healthy homosexual potential?

16. There seem to be very few happy heterosexuals. Techniques have been developed that might enable you to change if you really want to. Have you considered trying aversion therapy?

# Appendix H

*The following questionnaire is a tool that can spark discussion of myths and realities in workshops or classes and result in relearning.*

Answer each of the following questions on the following scale: 1—Always true, 2—Frequently true, 3—Occasionally or rarely true, 4—Never true.

1. Homosexuality is the most universally despised of all sexual behaviors.

2. Homosexuality is a criminal offense in the United States.

3. Lesbians prefer to imitate men in dress and mannerisms.

4. Most prostitutes are lesbians.

5. Homosexuals are a menace to society.

6. Homosexuals are born that way.

7. Homosexuals are more creative than heterosexuals.

8. Homosexuals are only found in urban areas.

9. Homosexuals hate members of the opposite sex.

10. Homosexuals are mentally ill.

11. Homosexuals are more sexually promiscuous than heterosexuals.

12. Homosexuals commit more crimes than heterosexuals.

13. Everyone is born heterosexual, but some people become homosexual because of being seduced by an older homosexual.

14. You can always tell homosexuals by the way they dress, talk, and act.

15. If a person is homosexual, no amount of motivation or therapy can change her/him.

16. Homosexuals can never become parents.

17. Boys raised by domineering mothers and weak (or absent) fathers usually become homosexual.

---

Questionnaire by Carol Tully.

18. Homosexuals are more inclined to molest children than are heterosexuals.

19. If a person has one or two same-sex sexual experiences she/he is homosexual.

20. The American Psychiatric Association states that homosexuality is a mental illness.

21. Homosexuals can be legally married in the United States.

22. Most homosexuals try to convert young people to homosexuality.

23. Children raised by homosexual parents (or homosexual people) usually become homosexual.

24. All homosexuals would become heterosexual if they found the right woman.

# Appendix I

*These open-ended sentences can be used by individuals and groups in clarifying their value orientations and homophobic feelings, attitudes, and practices. When these sentences are used as part of a staff training session, the group can be divided into small subgroups in which participants can discuss with each other their answers and feelings. The exercise might include reporting back from each subgroup to the total group.*

Where I work, an openly gay- or lesbian-identified (student, faculty, social worker) would...

The idea of viewing gay- or lesbian-identified people as healthy and "normal" seems...

In our agency, our response to an openly gay- or lesbian-identified employee is/would be...

If someone in my family fell in love with a member of the same sex and asked to talk with me about it, I would...

Children of gay- or lesbian-identified parents are likely to have problems with...

If I discovered that my 14-year-old client was sexually active with same-sex partners, my treatment approach would...

Gay or lesbian issues emerging within a family are destructive because...

The idea of comparing a committed same-sex relationship to a marriage feels...

Exercise by Carol Tully.

# Appendix J

In professional conferences and training sessions, the wearing of the pink triangle has become a way of calling people's attention to the oppression of gays and lesbians throughout history and to the immediate threat that the decade of the 1980s poses to the humanity of all. For learning purposes, groups can discuss the implications of the following statements for clients and lesbian and gay communities.

**The Pink Triangle, USA**

> "There will be no satanic churches, no more free distribution of pornography, no more abortion on demand, no more talk of rights for homosexuals. When the Christian majority takes control, pluralism will be seen as immoral and evil and the state will not permit anybody the right to practice evil." [Gary Potter, president of Catholics for Christian Political Action and a framer of the Family Protection Act]

> "No one is advocating the invasion of the private life of any individual," Ronald Reagan told interviewer Robert Scheer during the 1980 campaign. "I think Pat Campbell [sic] said it best in the trial of Oscar Wilde. She said, 'I have no objection to anyone's sex life as long as they don't practice it in the street and frighten the horses.'" This attitude did not prevent Reagan from assuring Scheer that he would never have signed a consenting adults bill as governor of California since "in the eyes of the lord, homosexuality is an abomination."

> Homosexuality is "one of those sins that could be coupled with murder...it would be the government that sits upon this land that would be executing homosexuals." [Dean Wycoff, head of Santa Clara County, California, Moral Majority]

> "While many church people are duped by their brainwashed, pink panty preachers into believing that we should merely pray for the homosexual, we feel that we must endorse and support the law of

God, which calls for the death penalty for homosexuals. It is not our intention to put this matter
up to discussion, or debate the matter, or start a
dialogue with a committee of queers as to their
rights of sexual freedom. The law of God states the
death penalty for homosexuals, and when God's
laws are again enforced, the death penalty is what
it will be." [Ku Klux Klan][1]

---

[1] Adapted by Hilda Hidalgo from quotes reported by Larry
Bush and Richard Goldstein, "Anti-Gay Backlash," *The Village Voice*
(New York City), April 8–14, 1981, pp. 10, 12, and 13. Reprinted
with permission of the reporters and the *Village Voice* © 1981.

# RESOURCES

# Introduction to Resources

**B** ecause this manual has been created as a response to professional mandates to enhance our knowledge about—and eliminate discrimination against—lesbians and gays, it would not be complete without as much information as can be conveniently included about and helpful to these potential clients. The material provided in the following subsections can be used both by professionals who wish simply to broaden their own knowledge base and by those whose clients can benefit from—if they do not desperately need—information about community resources, health-related organizations, hot lines, support networks, direct services and public benefits to which they may be entitled, and so on.

Two subsections, "Resources Related to Special Issues and Special Populations" and "References by Content Area," are further subdivided for the prospective reader's convenience. However, because many of the books and organizations cited are concerned with more than one aspect of the gay and lesbian community or with more than one problem, and because the demands of space require that some topics be combined, it is suggested that the reader browse through all the materials to get an overview of what is available.

Information is arranged under the following headings:

- Bibliographies
- Directories, Clearinghouses, Project Groups, and Miscellaneous Resources (Including Special Publications)
- Media Presentations and Other Teaching Aids
- Pamphlets and Packets: General
- Pamphlets and Packets: Legal Rights
- Resources Related to Special Issues and Populations
    - Aging
    - Alcoholism and Use of Other Drugs
    - Disabilities
    - Health Issues
    - Legal Issues
    - Parents of Lesbians or Gays
    - Religious and Spiritual Issues
    - Third World Media and Organizations

- References by Content Area
  Aging
  Alcoholism
  Disabilities
  Fiction and Personal Accounts
  Health Issues
  History and Politics
  Legal Issues
  Lesbian or Gay Couples
  Lesbian or Gay Parents
  Lesbians or Gays and Their Parents
  Third World
  Treatment and Professional Issues

There is much material concerning lesbian and gay issues that could not be included in this manual. For additional information on social work and its lesbian heritage, milestones for change, and homophobia in the helping professions, contact Committee on Lesbian and Gay Issues, National Association of Social Workers, Arizona Chapter, 610 West Broadway, Suite 103, Tempe, Ariz. 85281.

# Bibliographies

Council on Social Work Education. *An Annotated Bibliography of Lesbian and Gay Readings: 1st Edition.* 1983. Forty-one pages of references from books, articles in professional journals and other publications, pamphlets, and newspaper articles related to legal, civil rights, and general issues. Because of the proliferation of writing in this area, the Commission on Gay/Lesbian Issues in Social Work Education plans to update this bibliography on a regular basis. Address: 1744 R St., N.W., Washington, D.C. 20029.

———. For CSWE's bibliography of films, see entry under "Media Presentations and Other Teaching Aids."

Cruikshank, Margaret. *Lesbian Studies: Past and Present.* Old Westbury, N.Y.: Feminist Press, 1982. Thirty-five pages of books and articles "intended as a guide to instructors who wish to teach a course on lesbianism." However, because of its range, the book can be useful to helping professionals and as part of "bibliotherapy" with clients.

Heron, Ann. *One Teenager in Ten: Writings by Gay and Lesbian Youth.* Boston: Alyson Publications, 1983. Provides resources for parents and teenagers, including a letter exchange service for youths who cannot come out and communicate with peers close to home. Address: P.O. Box 2783, Boston, Mass. 02208.

Morin, Steve. "An Annotated Bibliography on Lesbians and Male Homosexuals (1967–74)." *JSAS Catalogue of Selected Documents in Psychology* (American Psychological Association), 1976, no. 15, MS. 1191.

———. "An Annotated Bibliography of Research on Lesbianism and Male Homosexuality (1967–74)." *JSAS Catalogue of Selected Documents in Psychology,* 1976, no. 15, MS. 1191.

National Association of Lesbian/Gay Alcoholism Professionals. *NALGAP Bibliography: Resources on Alcoholism and Lesbians/Gay Men.* 1985. Lists materials that are available from the files of the association. Includes organizational resources as well as films related to alcoholism. Address: 204 W. 20th St., New York, N.Y. 10011.

National Association of Lesbian and Gay Gerontology. As part of membership dues, provides updates in bibliographical references relative to aging lesbians and gays. Address: 1290 Sutter St., Suite 8, San Francisco, Calif. 94109.

National Gay Task Force. Has a variety of bibliographical listings available on particular topics. Recent emphasis has been on compiling information relative to AIDS. Address: 80 Fifth Ave., Suite 1601, New York, N.Y. 10011.

Oscar Wilde Memorial Bookshop. Publishes catalogue twice a year plus supplements. Address: 15 Christopher St., New York, N.Y. 10014, (212) 255-8097.

Out & Out Books. Publishing house specializing in issues relevant to feminist thought, including several lesbian titles. Catalogue (listing poetry, poetry magazines and anthologies, prose, books, pamphlets, articles, and record albums) available on request. Address: 476 Second St., Brooklyn, N.Y. 11215.

Paolella, Edward C. *An Annotated Gay/Lesbian Studies Bibliography.* Has particularly complete selections in the fields of Judaism and civil rights materials. Address: P.O. Box 480, Lenox Hill Station, New York, N.Y. 10021.

Parker, William. *Homosexuality: A Selective Bibliography of Over 3,000 Items.* Metuchen, N.J.: Scarecrow Press, 1971; and *Homosexuality Bibliography: Supplement, 1970–75,* 1977. These two extensive bibliographies (a total of 660 pages) include references to homosexuality in books and other literary works, theses and dissertations, newspaper and magazine articles (including the religious, popular, and homophile press), court cases, articles in scientific and medical journals, movies, television programs, audio/visual aids, pamphlets and documents, and U.S. laws applicable to consensual acts of adult homosexuals.

Stanley, Julia Penelope. "Bibliography of Lesbian Literature." Lists 103 entries of lesbian novels, poetry, source books, journals, and so forth, prepared for a course entitled, "Teaching Lesbian Novels: From Proposal to Reality." Available through Lesbian-Feminist Study Clearinghouse, 1012 Cathedral of Learning, University of Pittsburgh, Pittsburgh, Pa. 15260.

Weinberg, Martin S., and Bell, Allen P. *Homosexuality: An*

Annotated Bibliography. New York: Harper & Row, 1972 (550 pp., 1,263 items).

"The Whole Gay Catalogue." Listings of books in print published by and available from Lambda Rising, "the world's largest gay and lesbian bookstore." Address: 1625 Connecticut Ave., N.W., Washington, D.C. 20009, (202) 462-6969.

Womanbooks. Publishes a newsletter of book reviews. Address: 201 W. 92nd St., New York, N.Y. 10025.

Womanplace Bookstore. Provides a quarterly newsletter of annotated new and reissued publications. Address: 425 S. Mill Ave., Tempe, Ariz. 85281, (602) 966–9276.

# Directories, Clearinghouses, Project Groups, and Miscellaneous Resources (Including Special Publications)

*The Advocate,* 24 W. 39th St., New York, N.Y. 10014, (212) 869-9333. A national biweekly gay newspaper. Has published several articles on social services, health, and mental health problems within the lesbian and gay male communities. The following have been found useful:

> Issue 184, 25 February 1976, has an excellent report on "Alcoholism."

> Issue 188, 26 April 1976, has a controversial article on the facts about venereal disease in the gay community.

> Issue 192, 16 June 1976, has three perspectives on the problems of being gay and aging, entitled "Gay and Gray."

> Issue 207, 12 January 1977, "Hepatitis," an in-depth look at how this disease affects the gay community.

> Issue 208, 26 January 1977, "Gay Mental Health," discusses how finding a compatible therapist is a problem for gay people.

*Christopher Street Magazine* (literary and theoretical issues) and *The New York Native* (newspaper), 249 W. Broadway, New York, N.Y. 10013, (212) 925-8021.

Ferrari, Marianne. *Places of Interest—Gay Map Guide U.S.A. - Canada 1984.* A 200-page paperback filled with pertinent facts about bars, baths, hotels, services, clubs, religious organizations, women's groups, and other information of interest to gay/lesbian persons. Includes detailed maps for finding spots. Ferrari Publications, P.O. Box 35575, Phoenix, Ariz. 85011.

*Gayellow Pages.* New York: Renaissance House. Annual classified directory of gay/lesbian organizations, businesses,

and services in the U.S. and Canada. Also has three
regional editions for New York–New Jersey, the North-
east, and the South. Address: P.O. Box 292, Village Station, New York, N.Y. 10014, (212) 929-7720.

*The Homosexual Counseling Journal.* A quarterly journal of the
Homosexual Community Counseling Center, 30 E. 60th
St., New York, N.Y. 10022, (212) 688-0628. (This was
one of the first professional gay counseling centers for
gay and lesbian people and their families.) Especially
relevant articles are the following:

Vol. 1, no. 2 (April 1974)
"Family Therapy with the Homosexual: A Search"
"Counseling Concerns and Bisexual Behavior"

Vol. 1, no. 3 (July 1974)
"Gay Couple Counseling: Proceedings of a Conference"

Vol. 1, no. 4 (October 1974)
"Feminist Therapy with Lesbians and Other Women"

Vol. 2, no. 2 (April 1975)
"Teaching More-or-Less Straight Social Work Students
to Be More Helpful to More-or-Less Gay People"

Vol. 2, no. 3 (July 1975)
"Counseling and Homosexuality: Keynote Address of
the 1975 National Conference Series of the HCCC"
"Sexual Variations without Deviations"

Vol. 2, no. 4 (October 1975)
"A Study of Interpersonal Conflict in Homosexual Relations"

Vol. 3, no. 1 (January 1976)
"The Gay Addict in a Drug and Alcohol Abuse
Therapeutic Community"

Vol. 3, no. 2 (April 1976)
"Children in Gay Families: An Investigation of Services"
"Gay Service Organizations: A Survey"

*Journal of Homosexuality.* Copublished by Haworth Press, 28
E. 22nd St., New York, N.Y. 10010, and the Center for
Homosexual Education, Evaluation and Research, San
Francisco State University, 1600 Holloway Ave., San
Francisco, Calif. 94132. A quarterly refereed journal

devoted to empirical research (and its clinical implications) on lesbianism, male homosexuality, gender identity, and alternative lifestyles. Directed toward the audience of human service professionals.

*Journal of Social Issues,* 34, no. 3 (1978). "Special Issue on Psychology and the Gay Community," issue editors Dorothy Riddle and Stephen Morin. This collection of papers by members of the Association of Gay Psychologists is nonsexist, is totally nonhomophobic, and raises many important issues.

Lambda Legal Defense and Education Fund, Inc. Clearinghouse for legal information concerning gay/lesbian issues. Address: 132 W. 43rd St., New York, N.Y. 10036, (212) 944-9488.

Lesbian-Feminist Study Clearinghouse, Women's Studies Program. A nonprofit clearinghouse established in 1978 to foster and publicize the study of lesbian experience from a feminist perspective. Attempts to make available to the public a wide variety of lesbian feminist nonfiction writing and research that the popular press often rejects. Titles include unpublished manuscripts, conference papers, periodicals, and so forth. Catalog available on request. Address: 1012 Cathedral of Learning, University of Pittsburgh, Pittsburgh, Pa. 15260.

Mannion, Kristiann. *Female Homosexuals: A Comprehensive Review of Theory and Research,* MS. 1247, Journal Supplement Abstract Service of the American Psychological Association, 1976. APA Address: 1200 17th St., N.W., Washington, D.C. 20036.

*The National Gay Health Directory.* A compendium of health services for lesbians and gay men published by the National Gay Health Coalition, P.O. Box 677, Old Chelsea Station, New York, N.Y. 10011.

*Practice Digest,* 7 (Summer 1984). "Working with Gay and Lesbian Clients." Special issue of the quarterly publication of the National Association of Social Workers.

# Media Presentations and Other Teaching Aids

Council on Social Work Education. *Annotated Filmography of Selected Films with Lesbian/Gay Content.* 1984. Listings of educational films and distributors and feature-length films. Compiled by the Commission of Gay/Lesbian Issues in Social Work Education. Address: 1744 R St., N.W., Washington, D.C. 20029.

Deryck, Calderwood, and Szkodzinsky, Wasyl. *The Invisible Minority: The Homosexuals in Our Society.* Boston: Unitarian Universalist Association. Series of three sound filmstrips designed as an educational unit for lay groups or helping professionals who wish positive information on gay/lesbian persons. Discusses changing societal views and the purposes of the gay liberation movement. Includes interviews with many gay/lesbian persons, as well as authorities from religion, the helping professions, and law enforcement. Address: 25 Beacon St., Boston, Mass. 02108.

*Pink Triangles.* A 35-minute film comparing historical and contemporary examples of oppression (verbal, legal, governmental, and from helping professionals). Features counseling and health personnel in discussions of homophobia. Address: Cambridge Documentary Films, Inc., P.O. Box 385, Cambridge, Mass. 02139.

Unitarian Universalist Assocation. *About Your Sexuality.* 1983 revised edition. A multimedia (books, filmstrips, cassette tapes, activity booklets, and teacher's guide) educational course in human sexuality designed for persons of junior-high age and up. Includes frank, factual, explicit but sensitive, nonjudgmental information on birth control, masturbation, conception and childbirth, lovemaking, anatomy, homosexuality, venereal diseases, and so forth. Address: (see Deryck cited previously).

*Word Is Out* (see Appendix F).

# Pamphlets and Packets: General

*About Our Children.* Federation of Parents and Friends of Lesbians and Gays. Pamphlet (in English, Chinese, French, Japanese, and Spanish) describing this national self-help organization and offering helpful information and advice to parents of gays/lesbians. Address: P.O. Box 24565, Los Angeles, Calif. 90024, (213) 472-8952.

Blume, E. Sue. *Homosexuality Education and Linkage Programs (H.E.L.P) Package.* A training program and service development guide for helping professionals interested in better serving the lesbian and gay communities. Through a tape or lecture format, its unit syllabus covers topics of use to those working with lesbians and gay men; a selective bibliography keyed to the same topics; and a linkage component that informs practitioners of the variety of resources available to their clients in their communities, including social and political groups, self-help groups, professional organizations, crisis switchboards, bars, and bookstores. For further information and costs, write E. Sue Blume, CSW, P.O. Box 7167, Garden City, N.Y. 11530.

England, Michael E. *The Bible and Homosexuality.* Study guide to the biblical passages dealing with or having been interpreted as dealing with homosexuality. Thirty pages with bibliography. Address: Universal Fellowship of Metropolitan Community Churches, Department of Christian Social Action, P.O. Box 8835, Silver Spring, Md. 20910.

Gay Community Services Center. *Gay V.D.: Facts for Women and Men.* Extremely useful small pamphlet regarding venereal conditions found among gay or lesbian persons. Address: 1213 N. Highland Ave., Hollywood, Calif. 90038.

Gay Rights National Lobby. *If Your Constituents Ask. . . .* Billed as a "Self-Defense Kit" for politicians who are progay, this booklet includes suggestions for positive responses for critics, quotes from prominent religious organizations and community leaders, and an abbreviated list of denominations and organizations that support civil rights for the homosexually oriented. Address: P.O. Box 1892, Washington, D.C. 20013.

*Health and Venereal Disease Guide for Gay Men.* A 27-page booklet prepared by the Gay Men's Health Project, 74 Grove St., New York, N.Y. 10014.

Lee, Ron; Melleno, Frank; and Mullis, Robert. *Gay Men Speak.* San Francisco: Multi-Media Resource Center, 1973. Forty-two-page pamphlet.

*Lesbian Health Matters.* Available from the Santa Cruz Women's Health Center. More than 60 pages on gynecological issues, alcoholism and lesbians, health and sexuality, and more. Address: 250 Locust St., Santa Cruz, Calif. 95060.

National Gay Task Force. "Twenty Questions About Homosexuality." New York: National Gay Task Force, 1978. A useful pamphlet to distribute for educational and discussion purposes with lay groups. Address: 80 Fifth Ave., Suite 1601, New York, N.Y. 10011.

————. "About Coming Out." 1978.

New Ways Ministry. *Homosexual Catholics: A New Primer for Discussion* and a variety of other materials that present alternative approaches to traditional theology. Address: 4012 29th St., Mount Rainier, Md. 20712.

Wiesen-Cooke, Blanche. "Women Against Economic and Social Repression: The Two Front Challenge/Female Support Networks and Political Activism: Lillian Wald, Crystal Eastman, Emma Goldman and Jane Addams." The personal and professional lives of four early feminists (including figures contributing significantly to the rudimentary social philosophy that led to the establishment of the social work profession) are discussed. Attempts the restoration to the historical record of the various ways the loving natures of women—expressed interpersonally and through social action—were repressed by a heterosexist culture. Available through Out & Out Books, 476 Second St., Brooklyn, N.Y. 11215.

# Pamphlets and Packets: Legal Rights

Arthur, Christine (Psychiatrist), and English, Katherine (Attorney). "An Expert Testifies in a Lesbian Parenting Custody Case." Community Law Project. Address: 1628 Ankeny, S.E., Portland, Oreg. 97214.

Davies, Rosalie. *Motherright and the Lesbian.* Philadelphia: Custody Action for Lesbian Mothers, 1979. History, case histories, legal strategies, and counseling guidelines. Address: P.O. Box 281, Narberth, Pa. 19072.

Hitchens, Donna. *Lesbian Mother's Litigation Manual.* San Francisco: Lesbian Rights Project. Address: 1370 Mission St., 4th Floor, San Francisco, Calif. 94103, (415) 621-0675.

Hitchens, Donna J., and Thomas, Ann G. *Lesbian Mothers and Their Children: An Annotated Bibliography of Legal and Psychological Materials.* San Francisco: Lesbian Rights Project, November 1980. Excellent for legal defense.

Lambda Legal Defense and Education Fund, Inc. *AIDS Legal Guide: A Professional Resource on AIDS-Related Issues and Discrimination.* 1984. Address: 132 W. 43rd St., New York, N.Y. 10036, (212) 944-9488.

*Lesbians and Gay Men: The Law in Pennsylvania.* Philadelphia: American Civil Liberties Union, 1981. A resource on the law in Pennsylvania and valuable general text.

National Gay Task Force. *Gay Civil Rights Support Statements and Resolutions Packet.* Documents from professional, science, health, law, religion, and government groups. Address: 80 Fifth Ave., Suite 1601, New York, N.Y. 10011.

———. *Gay Parent's Support Packet.* Compilation of letters of support, articles, expert testimony, and relevant cases.

———. *Gay Teacher's Support Packet.* Statements on rights from professional groups, school boards, and so forth.

San Francisco–Bay Area National Lawyers Guild. *A Gay Parents' Legal Guide to Child Custody.* 1980. Prepared by the Anti-Sexism Committee. Address: 558 Capp St., San Francisco, Calif. 94110, (415) 285-5066.

———. *Gay Rights Skills Seminar Manual.* 2d ed. 1979. Prepared by the Gay Rights Task Force.

# Resources Related to Special Issues and Populations

Gay Forty Plus Club, P.O. Box 6741, San Francisco, Calif. **Aging**
94142.

Legacy, P.O. Box 11492, Chicago, Ill. 60611, (312) 275-3790;
(312) 883-1248.

Senior Action in a Gay Environment (SAGE), 208 W. 13th
St., New York, N.Y. 10011, (212) 741-2247.

Society for Senior Gay and Lesbian Citizens, Project Rainbow, 255 S. Hill St., Room 410, Los Angeles, Calif. 90012,
(213) 621-3180.

1. Call your local Alcoholics Anonymous (AA) or lesbian **Alcoholism**
or gay group for the gay or lesbian AA or gay Al-Anon near **and Use of**
you. An Alcoholics Together or Women for Sobriety chapter **Other Drugs**
might exist in your community, as well. Be advised, however,
that the AA member who answers the phone may not be
aware of the existence of gay AA, so you may have to inquire
further.

2. National Association of Gay Alcoholism Professionals
(NAGAP), 204 W. 20th St., New York, N.Y. 10011, (212)
807-0634.

3. Wisconsin Clearinghouse has a resource list. Address: 1954
E. Washington Ave., Madison, Wis. 53704.

4. The New York State Division of Substance Abuse Services, Narcotic and Drug Research Inc., Bureau of Training
and Resource Development, offers a three-day course on Gays
in Treatment. Open to all (including out-of-state) as space
is available. Address: 2 World Trade Center, Room 6701,
67th Floor, New York, N.Y. 10047, (212) 488-3662.

5. In many communities, lesbian or gay trainers or speakers
are available through local groups. If you need special qualifications (for example, familiarity with alcoholism), be sure
to screen the trainers or speakers.

6. Local lesbian, women's, and gay groups are aware of professionals such as doctors, lawyers, and therapists who are not biased and to whom clients can be referred. These professionals may themselves be lesbian or gay.

7. Some communities, particularly large cities, have facilities specifically for gay or lesbian drug or alcohol abusers.
For more information on these resources, consult *Gayellow Pages* (see "Directories..." section of this manual).

**Disabilities** Community Service Center for the Disabled. Counseling, peer groups, barrier removal. Address: 1295 University Ave., San Diego, Calif. 92103, (619) 293-3500.

Disability Rights Education and Defense Fund (DREDF), 2032 San Pablo Ave., Berkeley, Calif. 94702, (415) 644-2555 (within Calif.); (800) 227-2357 (outside Calif.).

Disabled Lesbian Alliance, Room 229, 5 University Place, New York, N.Y. 10003, (212) 580-3673.

Gay and Lesbian Community Services Center. Counseling, peer groups, consciousness and education, sign language classes. Address: 1213 N. Highland Ave., P.O. Box 38777, Los Angeles, Calif. 90038, (213) 464-7400.

Gay Social Services Project, Ville Marie Social Service Centre, Centre City Area Service Centre, 5 Weredale Park, Montreal, Quebec H3Z 1Y5, Canada, (514) 937-9581.

Independent Living Resource Center. Support group. Address: 4429 Cabrillo St., San Francisco, Calif. 94121, (415) 751-8765.

Lambda Resource Center for the Blind. Books and other materials on gay and lesbian themes on cassette tapes. Address: P.O. Box 1319, Chicago, Ill. 60690, (312) 274-0511.

National Rainbow Alliance of the Deaf, SCRDS. Over 18 chapters nationwide; gay and lesbian deaf social and advocacy group. Address: Box 1355, Burbank, Calif. 91507.

Operation Concern. Gay and Lesbian Counseling Service. Address: Pacific Medical Center, 1853 Market St., San Francisco, Calif. 94103, (415) 626-7000.

Para-Amps. Organization for physically disabled gay men. Address: P.O. Box 515, South Beloit, Ill. 61080.

Gay Men's Health Crisis, Inc., P.O. Box 274, 132 W. 24th **Health Issues**
St., New York, N.Y. 10011, (212) 807-6655.

National Coalition of Gay Sexually Transmitted Disease Services has recently published a pamphlet titled *Guidelines and Recommendations for Healthful Gay Sexual Activity.* 1984. Address: P.O. Box 239, Milwaukee, Wis. 53201, (414) 277-7671.

National Gay Health Coalition. Lesbian, gay, and bisexual caucuses of the major professional health-related organizations. Address: c/o Walter Lear, 206 N. 35th St., Philadelphia, Pa. 19104.

National Lesbian and Gay Health Foundation. This organization is in contact with a number of health-related groups and has been a leader in coordinating such organizations in efforts to "establish grassroots educational and service organizations" and networks on behalf of persons who have AIDS. Address: P.O. Box 65472, Washington Square Station, Washington, D.C. 20035.

Custody Action for Lesbian Mothers (CALM, Inc.), (litiga- **Legal Issues**
tion support service for lesbian mothers), P.O. Box 281, Narberth, Pa. 19072.

Gay Fathers Coalition, P.O. Box 50360, Washington, D.C. 20004.

Lambda Legal Defense and Education Fund, Inc., 132 W. 43rd St., New York, N.Y. 10036, (212) 944-9488.

Lesbian Mothers National Defense Fund, P.O. Box 21567, Seattle, Wash. 98111.

Federation of Parents and Friends of Lesbians and Gays **Parents of**
(Parents/FLAG), P.O. Box 24565, Los Angeles, Calif. 90024, **Lesbians or**
(213) 472-8952. **Gays**

National Federation of Parents and Friends of Gays. Not only can help in identifying local groups, but also provides a breadth of packets, pamphlets, and other materials that facilitate a positive approach to understanding a homosexual orientation. Address: 5715 16th St., N.W., Washington, D.C. 20011, (202) 726-3223.

**Religious and Spiritual Issues**  Many cities and college campuses have Metropolitan Community Churches that offer a nondenominational, Christian service for gays. Further information may be obtained from Metropolitan Community Church, 208 W. 13th St., New York, N.Y. 10011, (212) 242-1212; or 1050 S. Hill St., Los Angeles, Calif. 90015, (213) 748-0121.

Dignity is a resource for Roman Catholics who wish to retain affiliation with their religion. Because many Catholics are reluctant to contact their local parish priests, and because some diocesan centers refuse to provide information, counselors may need to obtain information from Dignity–National, 355 Boylston, Boston, Mass. 02116.

For Episcopalians, there is Integrity, which serves purposes that are comparable to Dignity's. If the diocesan office has no information, contact Integrity/San Francisco, P.O. Box 6444, San Francisco, Calif. 94150, (408) 268-3378.

Helping professionals should seek out spiritual resources and assess attitudes of local religious facilities for clients. Through such exploration, clients can avoid rejection and have meaningful experiences. For example, New York City has a Gay Synagogue; Washington, D.C., has the Unitarian Gay Community as part of the All Souls Unitarian Church; and Lutherans Concerned for Gay People functions in Los Angeles, Chicago, and some other cities. Phoenix has an "underground" Mormon group that can be located through the Lesbian and Gay Assistance and Information Line in that city.

**Third World Media and Organizations***  Azalea Magazine and Collective, (Third World women), 306 Lafayette Ave., Brooklyn, N.Y. 11238.

Blacklight (monthly newsletter), P.O. Box 56255, Brightwood Station, Washington, D.C. 20001.

Colored Voices (Third World lesbians), 304 11th St., Seattle, Wash. 98102, (206) 329-9862.

---

*Some of these media and organizations are not totally lesbian and gay or not totally Third World. Most have significant lesbian and gay representation and are strong advocates for lesbian and gay rights as well as Third World issues.

Committee for Black and Third World Health Professionals, c/o NCBG, P.O. Box 548, Columbia, Md. 21045, (202) 797-8877.

Debreta's (Third World women), P.O. Box 4232, Inglewood, Calif. 90302, (213) 641-4650.

Gay Insurgent (socialist publication), P.O. Box 2337, Philadelphia, Pa. 19103.

Freedom Socialist Party, 32 Union Square E., #307, New York, N.Y. 10003, (212) 677-7002.

Freedom Socialist Party (newspaper), 3815 Fifth Ave., N.E., Seattle, Wash. 98105, (206) 632-7449.

Jemima (black lesbian writers), 314 E. 9th St., #5-E, New York, N.Y. 10028.

Lesbians of Color, c/o Women's Resource Program, P.O. Box 38777, Los Angeles, Calif. 90038.

Lesbians of Color, P.O. Box 5077, San Diego, Calif. 92105, (714) 284-7347.

NGTF Third World Lesbian and Gay Caucus, 80 Fifth Ave., Suite 1601, New York, N.Y. 10011, (212) 741-5800.

Oakland Black and Third World Gays, 5960 Racine St., Oakland, Calif. 94609, (415) 654-7818.

OMBAHEE River Collective (Third World lesbian feminists), 149 Windsor St., #3, Cambridge, Mass. 02139, (617) 661-4104.

Oregon Women's Land Trust, P.O. Box 1692, Roseberg, Oreg. 97470, (503) 679-4655.

Philadelphia Lesbian and Gay Task Force, 3601 Cherry St., Philadelphia, Pa. 19102, (215) 563-9584.

Radical Women, 3815 Fifth Ave., N.E., Seattle, Wash. 98105, (206) 632-7449.

Salsa Soul Sisters (Third World women), c/o Washington Square Methodist Church, 133 W. 4th St., New York, N.Y. 10012, (212) 273-0995.

Third World Coalition, American Friends Service Committee (Quakers), 1501 Cherry St., Philadelphia, Pa. 19102, (215) 241-7034.

Third World Feminist Collective, 2562 Arunah Ave., Baltimore, Md. 21216, (301) 945-2854.

Third World Gay Coalition, c/o Pacific Center for Human Growth, P.O. Box 908, Berkeley, Calif. 94701, (415) 548-8283.

Third World Gay/Lesbian Counseling Program, c/o Operation Concern, Pacific Medical Center, 1853 Market St., San Francisco, Calif. 94103, (415) 626-7000.

Third World Lesbian and Gay Caucus of the National March on Washington, 943 Ninth St., N.W., Washington, D.C. 20001, (202) 789-1070.

Third World Lesbian/Gay Conference, P.O. Box 548, Columbia, Md. 21045, (202) 797-8877.

Third World Lesbian/Gay Task Force, P.O. Box 59096, Los Angeles, Calif. 90059, (213) 751-3429.

Women's Land, c/o Medicine Wheel, P.O. Box 2189, St. John, Ariz. 85936.

WXPN Third World News, 3905 Spruce St., Philadelphia, Pa. 19104, (215) 387-5401.

# References by Content Area

Berger, Raymond M. *Gay and Gray: The Older Homosexual Man.* **Aging**
Urbana: University of Illinois Press, 1982. Boston: Alyson Publications, 1984.

———. "Psychological Adaptation of the Older Male Homosexual," *Journal of Homosexuality,* 5 (Spring 1980), pp. 161–175.

———. "Realities of Gay and Lesbian Aging," *Social Work,* 29 (January–February 1984), pp. 57–62.

———. "The Unseen Minority: Older Gays and Lesbians," *Social Work,* 27 (May 1982), pp. 236–242.

Barracks, Barbara, and Jarratt, Kent, eds. *Sage Writings from the Lesbian and Gay Men's Writing Workshop at Senior Action in a Gay Environment.* New York: Teachers & Writers Collaborative, 1980.

Bataya. "The Spectrum of Lesbian Experience: Age," in Ginny Vida, ed., *Our Right to Love: A Lesbian Resource Book.* Englewood Cliffs, N.J.: Prentice-Hall, 1978.

Catalano, Donald J., Valentine, William E., and Greever, Lee. "Social Services for Aging Gay Men," *Catalyst,* 12 (December 1981), pp. 47–60.

Dlugos, Tim. "Gay Widows: Your Lover Just Died and the Family Arrives to Take Everything," *Christopher Street* (New York City), 4, no. 6 (1980), pp. 23–24.

Fenwick, R. D. "Perspectives on Aging." *The Advocate Guide to Gay Health.* New York: E. P. Dutton & Co., 1978. Chapter 6.

Francher, J. Scott and Henkin, Janet. "The Menopausal Queen: Adjusting to Aging and the Male Homosexual," *American Journal of Orthopsychiatry,* 43 (July 1973), pp. 670–674.

Friend, Richard A. "GAYging: Adjustment and the Older Gay Male," *Alternative Lifestyles,* 3 (May 1980), pp. 231–248.

Gidlow, Elsa. "A View from the Seventy-Seventh Year," *Women: A Journal of Liberation,* 4, no. 4 (1977–78), pp. 32–35.

Kelly, James J. "The Aging Male Homosexual: Myth and Reality," in Martin Levine, ed., *Gay Men: The Sociology of Male Homosexuality.* New York: Harper & Row, 1979. Reprinted from *Gerontologist,* 17 (August 1977), pp. 328–332.

———. "Homosexuality and Aging," in Judd Marmor, ed., *Homosexual Behavior: A Modern Reappraisal.* New York: Basic Books, 1980.

Kelly, James J., and Johnson, Myra T. "Deviate Sex Behavior in the Aging: Social Definitions and the Lives of Older Gay People," in Oscar J. Kaplan, ed., *Psychopathology and Aging* (New York: Academic Press, 1979).

Kimmel, Douglas C. "Adjustment to Aging Among Gay Men," in Betty Berzon and Robert Leighton, eds., *Positively Gay.* Millbrae, Calif.: Celestial Arts Publishing Co., 1979.

———. "Adult Development and Aging: A Gay Perspective," *Journal of Social Issues,* 34, no. 3 (1978), pp. 113–130.

———. "Life-History Interviews of Aging Gay Men," *International Journal of Aging and Human Development,* 10, no. 3 (1979–80), pp. 239–248.

———. "Psychotherapy and the Older Gay Man," *Psychotherapy: Theory, Research and Practice,* 14 (Winter 1977), pp. 386–393.

Kleinberg, Seymour. *Alienated Affections: Being Gay in America.* New York: St. Martin's Press, 1980.

Laner, Mary Riege. "Growing Older Female: Heterosexual and Homosexual," *Journal of Homosexuality,* 4 (Spring 1979), pp. 267–275.

———. "Growing Older Male: Heterosexual and Homosexual," *Gerontologist,* 18 (1978), pp. 496–501.

Martin, Del, and Lyon, Phyllis. "The Older Lesbian," in Betty Berzon and Robert Leighton, eds., *Positively Gay.* Millbrae, Calif.: Celestial Arts Publishing Co., 1979.

Minnigerode, Fred A. "Age-Status Labeling in Homosexual Men," *Journal of Homosexuality,* 1, no. 3 (1976), pp. 273–276.

Minnigerode, Fred A., and Adelman, Marcy R. "Elderly Homosexual Women and Men: Report on a Pilot Study," *Family Coordinator,* 27 (October 1978), pp. 451–456.

Raphael, Sharon M. and Robinson, Mina K. "The Older Lesbian: Love Relationships and Friendship Patterns," *Alternative Lifestyles,* 3 (May 1980), pp. 207–229.

Weinberg, Martin S. "The Aging Male Homosexual," *Medical Aspects of Human Sexuality,* 3 (December 1969), pp. 66–72.

———. "The Male Homosexual: Age-Related Variations in Social and Psychological Characteristics," *Social Problems,* 17, no. 4 (1970), pp. 527–537.

**Alcoholism**

Sandmaier, Marian. *The Invisible Alcoholics: Women and Alcohol Abuse.* New York: McGraw-Hill Book Co., 1980. Personal, social, and political issues necessary for understanding lesbian alcoholics.

Swallow, Jean, ed. *Out from Under: Sober Dykes and Our Friends.* San Francisco: Spinsters, Ink, 1983. The experience of the recovering lesbian alcoholic and those close to her.

Ziebold, Thomas O., and Mongeon, John E. *Alcoholism and Homosexuality.* New York: Haworth Press, 1982. Mostly concerns alcoholism in gay men, with good general analysis of the issues.

**Disabilities**

Berenstein, Frederick. "The Homosexual Retardate: Theory and Group Work," *Journal for Special Educators of the Mentally Retarded,* 9 (Winter 1973), pp. 74–79.

Blumenfeld, Warren. "Gay and Blind," *Gay Community News,* 12 April 1980, p. 10.

Giteck, Lenny. "The Dilemma of Double Discrimination," *The Advocate* (San Mateo, Calif.), 17 May 1978, pp. 14–17.

Gochros, Harvey L., and Gochros, Jean S., eds. *The Sexually Oppressed.* New York: Follett Publishing Co., Association Press, 1977.

Oberon, Paul Wesley. "Sign Me Gay: The Double Challenge of the Deaf," *Ten Percent* (U.C.L.A., Los Angeles) 2, no. 3 (February 1981), p. 5.

*Off Our Backs* (Washington, D.C.) 11, no. 5 (May 1981). "Special Issue: Women with Disabilities."

Sex and Disability Project. *Who Cares? A Handbook on Sex Education and Counseling Services for Disabled People.* Washington, D.C.: George Washington University, 1979.

Twyford, Neal. "The Double Closet, Disabled Gays Who Cope with Coming Out—Twice," *The Advocate* (San Mateo, Calif.), Issue 336, 18 February 1982.

Witomski, T. R. "Handicapped Gays: The Search for Accepance," *Blueboy* (New York City), April 1980, p. 79.

Zakarewsky, George T. "Patterns of Support among Gay Lesbian Deaf Persons," *Sexuality and Disability,* 2 (Fall 1979), pp. 178–191.

**Fiction and Personal Accounts**

Adair, Nancy, and Adair, Casey. *Word Is Out: Stories of Some of Our Lives.* New York: Dell Publishing Co., 1978.

*And God Bless Uncle Harry and His Roommate Jack, Who We Are Not Supposed to Talk About.* New York: Avon Books, 1978.

Brown, Rita Mae. *Rubyfruit Jungle.* Plainfield, Vt.: Daughters, 1973. New York: Bantam Books, 1977.

Gantz, Joe. *Whose Child Cries: Children of Gay Parents Talk about Their Lives.* Rolling Hills Estates, CA: Jalmar Press, 1983.

Gearhart, Sally M. *The Wanderground: Stories of the Hill Women.* 2d ed. Watertown, Mass.: Persephone Press, 1979.

Kleinberg, Seymour, ed. *The Other Persuasion: An Anthology of Short Fiction about Gay Men and Women.* New York: Vintage Trade Books, 1977.

Lorde, Audre. *Zami: A New Spelling of My Name.* Watertown, Mass.: Persephone Press, 1982.

Millett, Kate. *Sita.* New York: Ballantine Books, 1977.

Rule, Jane. *Lesbian Images.* New York: Doubleday & Co., 1975.

Tripp, C. A. *The Homosexual Matrix.* New York: McGraw-Hill Book Co., 1975.

Warren, Patricia N. *The Front Runner.* New York: William Morrow & Co., 1974.

White, Edmund. *A Boy's Own Story.* New York: E. P. Dutton & Co., 1982.

**Health Issues**

Berger, Raymond M. "Health Care for Lesbians and Gay Men: What Social Workers Should Know," *Journal of Social Work and Human Sexuality,* 1 (Spring 1983), pp. 59–73.

Brooks, Virginia. *Minority Stress and Lesbian Women.* Lexington, Mass.: Lexington Books, 1981.

Centers for Disease Control. "Update: AIDS in the U.S.," *Morbidity and Mortality Weekly Report,* 32, no. 2. Atlanta,

Ga.: Public Health Service, U.S. Department of Health & Human Services, January 6, 1984.

Fenwick, R. D. *The Advocate Guide to Gay Health.* New York: E. P. Dutton & Co., 1978. Oriented for gay men, with chapters on transmission, diagnosis, and treatment of sexually transmitted diseases (STD).

Kassler, Jeanne. *Gay Men's Health: A Guide to the AID Syndrome and Other Sexually Transmitted Diseases.* New York: Harper & Row, 1983. The first book on AIDS with a breakdown of current theories, and categorized descriptions of STDs.

McGahee, Glenn. *Personal Advocacy for People with AIDS and AIDS Related Complex.* Atlanta, Ga.: AID Atlanta, 1984. Positive suggestions for living with AIDS from a person who is doing just that.

*National Gay Health Directory: A Compendium of Health Services for Lesbians and Gay Men.* Compiled by Caitlin Conor Ryan and Jeanne Brossart. New York: National Lesbian and Gay Health Foundation, 1979, 1980, 1983. State-by-state listings of lesbian- and gay-oriented health practitioners, therapists, clinics, and facilities.

O'Donnell, Mary, et al. *Lesbian Health Matters!* Santa Cruz, Calif.: Santa Cruz Women's Health Collective, 1979. Sections on health and sexuality, alcoholism, menopause, alternative fertilization, and feminist therapy.

*Sourcebook on Lesbian/Gay Health Care.* New York: National Lesbian and Gay Health Foundation, 1984. Handbook from the International Lesbian/Gay Health Conference listing all workshops presented, essays on lesbian and gay health, AIDS resources, and health services and organizations.

**History and Politics**

Addams, Jane. *My Friend, Julia Lathrop.* New York: Macmillan Co., 1935.

————. *Women at the Hague.* New York: Macmillan Co., 1915.

Berube, A. "Coming Out Under Fire," *Mother Jones,* February–March 1983.

Boswell, John. *Christianity, Social Tolerance, and Homosexuality: Gay People in Western Europe from the Beginning of the Christian Era to the Fourteenth Century.* Chicago: University of Chicago Press, 1980.

Brooks, Gladys. *Three Wise Virgins.* New York: E. P. Dutton & Co., 1957.

Bullough, Vern L. *Sexual Variance in Society and History.* Chicago: University of Chicago Press, 1980.

Davis, Allen F. *American Heroine: The Life and Legend of Jane Addams.* New York: Oxford University Press, 1973.

*The Family,* 9 (February 1929), pp. 319–359. "Memorial Issue for Mary E. Richmond."

Farrell, John C. *Beloved Lady: A History of Jane Addams' Ideas on Reform and Peace.* Baltimore, Md.: Johns Hopkins University Press, 1967.

*Frontiers, A Journal of Women's Studies,* 4, no. 3 (Fall 1979). "Lesbian History Issue."

Goodman, Bernice. *The Lesbian: A Celebration of Difference.* Brooklyn, N.Y.: Out & Out Books, 1977.

Greenstone, J. David. "Dorothea Dix and Jane Addams: From Transcendentalism to Pragmatism in American Social Reform," *Social Service Review,* 53 (December 1979), pp. 527–559.

James, Edward T., James, Janet Wilson, and Boyer, Paul S., eds. *Notable American Women 1607–1950.* Cambridge, Mass.: Harvard University Press, Belknap Press, 1971.

Katz, Jonathan. *Gay American History: Lesbians and Gay Men in the U.S.A., a Documentary.* New York: Thomas Y. Crowell Co., 1976.

———. *Gay-Lesbian Almanac.* New York: Harper & Row, 1983.

Lenroot, Katharine F. "Grace Abbott and the Children's Bureau," *The Child,* 2 (August 1939), pp. 29–31.

Mahaffey, Maryann. "Ladylike Charity in a Gentleman's World." Speech delivered at "Social Work Practice in Sexist Society: First NASW Conference on Social Work Practice with Women." Washington, D.C., 15 September 1980.

Marmor, Judd. *Homosexual Behavior: A Modern Reappraisal.* New York: Basic Books, 1980.

Marshall, Helen E. *Dorothea Dix.* Chapel Hill: University of North Carolina Press, 1937.

Milkstein, Beth, and Bodin, Jeanne. *We, the American Women.* Chicago: Science Research Associates, 1977.

Parris, Guichard, and Brooks, Lester. *Blacks in the City.* Boston: Little, Brown & Co., 1971.

Perkins, Frances. "My Recollections of Florence Kelley," *Social Service Review*, 28 (March 1954), pp. 12–19.

Rich, Margaret E. "Zilpha Drew Smith," *The Family*, 2 (May 1939), pp. 67–79.

Robinson, Virginia P., ed. *Jessie Taft, Therapist and Social Work Educator*. Philadelphia: University of Pennsylvania Press, 1962.

Sahli, Nancy. "Smashing: Women's Relationships Before the Fall," *Chrysalis*, no. 8 (1979), pp. 17–27.

Scudder, Vida Dutton. *On Journey*. New York: E. P. Dutton & Co., 1984.

Smith-Rosenberg, Caroll. "The Female World of Love and Ritual: Relations between Women in Nineteenth-Century America," *Signs*, 1 (Autumn 1975), pp. 1–29.

Vandiver, Susan T. "A Herstory of Women in Sex," *Women's Issues and Sex Practice* (1980), pp. 21–38.

Weiss, Nancy J. *The National Urban League*. New York: Oxford University Press, 1974.

Wiesen-Cook, Blanche. "Female Support Networks and Political Activism: Lillian Wald, Crystal Eastman, and Emma Goldman," *Chrysalis*, 3 (1977), pp. 43–61.

Willard, Frances E. *Glimpses of Fifty Years: The Autobiography of an American Woman*. Chicago, 1889.

Willard, Frances E., and Livermore, Mary A., eds. *Women of the Century*. Buffalo, N.Y.: Charles Wells Moulton, 1893.

Wilson, Dorothy Clarke. *Stranger and Traveler*. Boston: Little Brown & Co., 1978.

Wisner, Elizabeth. "Edith Abbott's Contributions to Social Work Education," *Social Service Review*, 32 (March 1958), pp. 1–10.

Wright, Helen R. "Three Against Time: E. and G. Abbott and Sophonisba P. Breckenridge," *Social Service Review*, 28 (March 1954), pp. 41–53.

Wysor, Bettie. *The Lesbian Myth: Insights and Conversations*. New York: Random House, 1974.

**Legal Issues**

"The Avowed Lesbian Mother and Her Right to Child Custody: A Constitutional Challenge that Can No Longer Be Denied," Law Note, 12 *San Diego Law Review* 799, 820 (1975).

Bernstein, Barton E. "Legal and Social Interface in Counseling Homosexual Clients," *Social Casework,* 58 (January 1977), pp. 36–40.

Boggan, E. Carrington, et al. *The Rights of Gay People.* New York: Bantam Books, 1983.

Curry, Hayden, and Clifford, Denis. *A Legal Guide for Gay and Lesbian Couples.* Reading, Mass.: Addison-Wesley Publishing Co., 1980. An excellent resource book for most areas.

Hitchens, Donna. "Social Attitudes, Legal Standards and Personal Trauma in Child Custody Cases," *Journal of Homosexuality,* 5 (1979), p. 89.

Hitchens, D.; Martin, D.; and Morgan, M. "An Alternative View to Child Custody: When One Parent Is a Homosexual," *Conciliation Courts Review,* 17 (1979), p. 27.

Hunter, Nan, and Polikoff, Nancy. "Custody Rights of Lesbian Mothers: Legal Theory and Litigation Strategy," 25 *Buffalo Law Review* 691 (1976).

**Lesbian or Gay Couples**

Ables, Billie S. *Therapy for Couples.* San Francisco: Jossey-Bass, 1977.

Berzon, Betty, and Leighton, Robert, eds. *Positively Gay.* Millbrae, Calif.: Celestial Arts Publishing Co., 1979. A collection of essays on new approaches in gay life to such issues as family relationships, mental health, couples, and aging.

Brooks, Virginia. *Minority Stress and Lesbian Women.* Lexington, Mass.: D. C. Heath & Co., 1981.

Clark, Don. *Loving Someone Gay.* Millbrae, Calif.: Celestial Arts Publishing Co., 1977. New York: New American Library, Signet Books, 1978. A gay therapist offers sensitive, intelligent guidance to gays, their friends, families, and therapists who want to be supportive.

Decker, Beverly. "Counseling Gay and Lesbian Couples," *Journal of Social Work and Human Sexuality,* 2 (Winter 1983–Spring 1984). Special double issue, "Homosexuality and Social Work."

Di Bella, G. "Family Psychotherapy with the Homosexual Family: A Community Psychiatry Approach to Homosexuality," *Community Mental Health Journal,* 4 (1979).

Litwok, Evelyn; Weber, Rose; Rux, Julia; DeForest, Joan; and Davis, Rosalie. *Considerations in Therapy with Lesbian Clients.* Proceedings of Symposium Presented at 1978 Midwinter Conference of Association for Women in Psychology, Pittsburgh, Pa. Philadelphia: Women's Resources/Omega Press, 1979.

*Loving Women.* 2d ed. Sonora, Calif.: The Nomadic Sisters, 1976. An illustrated lesbian sexuality book.

Moses, A. Elfin, and Hawkins, Robert O., Jr. *Counseling Lesbian Women and Gay Men: A Life-Issues Approach.* St. Louis, Mo.: C. V. Mosby Co., 1982.

Sager, Clifford J. *Marriage Contracts and Couple Therapy.* New York: Brunner/Mazel, 1976.

Silverstein, Charles. *Man to Man: Gay Couples in America.* William Morrow & Co., 1981.

Silverstein, Charles, and White, Edmund. *The Joy of Gay Sex.* New York: Simon & Schuster, 1977. Illustrated guidebook for enhancing sexual and loving relationships for gay men. Also serves as a good dictionary for heterosexuals working with gay men.

Sisley, Emily L. and Harris, Bertha. *The Joy of Lesbian Sex.* New York: Simon & Schuster, 1978.

Vida, Ginny, ed. *Our Right to Love: A Lesbian Resource Book.* Englewood Cliffs, N.J.: Prentice-Hall, 1978. A comprehensive lesbian resource book; contains articles, personal testimony, photographs, and many lists of resources.

Woodman, Natalie Jane. "Social Work with Lesbian Couples," in Ann Weick and Susan T. Vandiver, eds., *Women, Power, and Change.* Selected Papers from Social Work Practice in Sexist Society: First NASW Conference on Social Work Practice with Women. Washington, D.C.: National Association of Social Workers, 1982.

Woodman, Natalie Jane, and Lenna, Harry R. *Counseling with Gay Men and Women: A Guide for Facilitating Positive Life-Styles.* San Francisco: Jossey-Bass, 1980. See especially chapter 7, which focuses on interpersonal relations.

**Lesbian or Gay Parents**

Bozett, Frederick W. "Gay Fathers: Evolution of the Gay-Father Identity," *American Journal of Orthopsychiatry,* 51 (July 1981), pp. 552–559.

Goodman, Bernice. "The Lesbian Mother," *American Journal of Orthopsychiatry*, 43 (March 1973), p. 283.

————. "Some Mothers Are Lesbians," in Elaine Norman and Arlene Mancuso, eds., *Women's Issues in Social Work Practice*. Itasca, Ill.: F. E. Peacock, Publishers, 1980. Describes trials and traumas of lesbian mothers.

Green, R. "Sexual Identity of 37 Children Raised by Homosexual or Trans-sexual Parents," *American Journal of Psychiatry*, 135 (1978), p. 692.

Hoeffer, Beverly. "Children's Acquisition of Sex-Role Behavior in Lesbian-Mother Families," *American Journal of Orthopsychiatry*, 51 (July 1981), pp. 536–544.

Kirkpatrick, Martha; Smith, Catherine; Roy, Ron. "Lesbian Mothers and Their Children: A Comparative Survey," *American Journal of Orthopsychiatry*, 51 (July 1981), pp. 545–551.

Lewin, E. "Lesbianism and Motherhood: Implications for Child Custody," *Human Organization*, 40 (1981).

Lewis, Karen Gail. "Children of Lesbians: Their Point of View," *Social Work*, 25 (May 1980), pp. 198–203.

Mucklow, B., and Phelan, K. "Lesbian and Traditional Mothers' Responses to Adult Response to Child Behavior and Self-Concept," *Psychological Reports*, 44 (1979), p. 880.

Rees, R. "A Comparison of Children of Lesbian and Single Heterosexual Mothers on Three Measures of Socialization," *Dissertation Abstracts International* (1979).

**Lesbians or Gays and Their Parents**

Borhek, Mary V. *Coming Out to Parents: A Two-Way Survival Guide for Lesbians and Gay Men and Their Parents*. New York: Pilgrim Press, 1983.

Fairchild, Betty, and Hayward, Nancy. *Now That You Know: What Every Parent Should Know about Homosexuali'* New York: Harcourt Brace Jovanovich, 1981. Parents of gays offer valuable insights and advice.

Hanckel, Frances, and Cunningham, John. *A Way of Love, A Way of Life: A Young Person's Introduction to What It Means to Be Gay*. New York: Lothrop, Lee, Shepard Books, 1979. Articles on various aspects of lesbian and gay lifestyles from a white middle-class perspective.

Morin, S. F., and Schutz, S. J. "The Gay Movement and

the Rights of Children," *Journal of Social Issues,* 34 (1978), pp. 137–148. Principles for serving the needs of homosexual youths before identification becomes difficult.

Shilts, Randy. "Gay Youth, the Lonely Young," *The Advocate,* 1 June 1977.

Silverstein, Charles. *A Family Matter: A Parent's Guide to Homosexuality.* New York: McGraw-Hill Book Co., 1978. Sketches of several middle-class families dealing with gay members. A good "first book" for parents.

Stanley, Julia Penelope, and Wolfe, Susan J., eds. *The Coming Out Stories.* Watertown, Mass.: Persephone Press, 1980. A collection of essays recounting efforts of lesbians during various stages of coming out.

Steinhorn, Audrey I. "Lesbian Adolescents in Residential Treatment," *Social Casework,* 60 (October 1979).

Woodman, Natalie Jane, and Lenna, Harry R. *Counseling with Gay Men and Women: A Guide for Facilitating Positive Life-Styles.* San Francisco: Jossey-Bass, 1980. Chapter 6 deals specifically with helping youthful lesbians and gays.

*Young, Gay and Proud.* Boston, Mass: Alyson Publications, 1980. A comprehensive book that deals with most aspects of coming out.

## Third World

Hidalgo, Hilda. "The Puerto Rican Lesbian in the United States," in Trudey E. Darty and Sandee J. Potter, eds. *Women-Identified, Women Anthology.* Palo Alto, Calif.: Mayfield Publishing Co., 1984.

———. "Third World Lesbians: Organizing at the National Level to Combat Oppression," in Frederique Delacoste and Felice Neuman, eds., *Fight Back.* Minneapolis, Minn.: Eleis Press, 1982.

Lourdes, Arguelles, and Rich, B. Ruby. "Homosexuality, Homophobia and Revolution: Notes Toward an Understanding of the Cuban Lesbian and Gay Experience," *Signs,* The Lesbian Issue, 9 (Summer 1984).

## Treatment and Professional Issues

Bell, Alan P. et al. *Sexual Preference: Its Development in Men and Women.* Bloomington: Indiana University Press, 1981.

Berger, Raymond M. "What Is a Homosexual? A Definitional Model," *Social Work,* 28 (March–April 1983), pp. 132–135.

Berger, Raymond M., and Kelly, James J. "Do Social Work Agencies Discriminate against Homosexual Job Applicants?" *Social Work,* 26 (May 1981), pp. 193–198.

Cass, Vivienne. "Homosexual Identity Formation: A Theoretical Model," *Journal of Homosexuality,* 4 (Spring 1979).

Clark, Don. *Living Gay.* Millbrae, Calif.: Celestial Arts Publishing Co., 1979.

Cummerton, Joan M. "Homophobia and Social Work Practice with Lesbians," in Ann Weick and Susan T. Vandiver, eds., *Women, Power, and Change.* Selected Papers from Social Work Practice in Sexist Society: First NASW Conference on Social Work Practice with Women, Washington, D.C., 14–16 September 1980. Washington, D.C.: National Association of Social Workers, 1982.

Dulaney, Diana D., and Kelly, James. "Improving Services to Gay and Lesbian Clients," *Social Work,* 27 (March 1982), pp. 178–183.

Gonsiorek, John. "Psychological Adjustment and Homosexuality," *JSAS Catalog of Selected Documents in Psychology* (American Psychological Association), 7, no. 2 (1977), p. 45, MS. 1478.

Goodman, Bernice. *Confronting Homophobia.* New York: National Gay Health Coalition Educational Foundation, 1978.

———. *"Where Will You Be?" The Professional Oppression of Gay People: A Lesbian/Feminist Perspective.* West Hempstead, N.Y.: Woman Made Products, 1980.

Gramick, Jeannine. "Homophobia: A New Challenge," *Social Work,* 28 (March–April 1983), pp. 137–141.

Jay, Karla, and Young, Allen. *The Gay Report.* New York: Summit Books, 1979.

Kinsey, Alfred C.; Pomeroy, Wardell B.; and Martin, Clyde E. *Sexual Behavior in the Human Male.* Philadelphia: W. B. Saunders Co., 1948.

Kinsey, Alfred C., et al. *Sexual Behavior in the Human Female.* Philadelphia: W. B. Saunders Co., 1953.

Lewis, Lou Ann. "The Coming-Out Process for Lesbians: Integrating a Stable Identity," *Social Work,* 29 (September–October 1984), pp. 464–469.

Liljestrand, P.; Gerlig, E.; and Saliba, P.A. "The Effects of Social Sex-Role Stereotypes and Sexual Orientation on Psychotherapeutic Outcomes," *Journal of Homosexuality,* 3 (1978), pp. 361–372.

Masters, William H., and Johnson, Virginia. *Homosexuality in Perspective.* Boston: Little, Brown & Co., 1979.

Money, John. *Love and Love Sickness: The Science of Sex, Gender, Difference, and Pair Bonding.* Baltimore, Md.: Johns Hopkins University Press, 1980.

Shernoff, Michael J. "Family Therapy for Lesbian and Gay Clients," *Social Work,* 29 (July–August 1984), pp. 393–396.

# About the Editors and Authors

**Editors** **Hilda Hidalgo** is a professor of social work and urban planning at Rutgers, the State University of New Jersey. She holds a PhD in social planning, an MSW in clinical social work, and an MA in guidance and counseling. Dr. Hidalgo is an ACSW member and a licensed marriage counselor in New Jersey. She has authored *The Puerto Ricans in New Jersey; Ethnic Differences that Make a Difference in the Delivery of Rehabilitation Services to Puerto Ricans;* "Facilitating Cultural Pluralism in Performance Based Teacher Education Programs: The Administrator's Role"; and "Counseling Inner City Adults to Start Higher Education." Dr. Hidalgo has served as commissioner for CSWE on the Minority Commission, first vice-president of the New Jersey Chapter of NASW, and a member of the National NASW Task Force on Lesbian and Gay Issues.

**Travis L. Peterson** is a private practitioner specializing in gay and lesbian issues. He holds an MSW degree and is a certified social worker–advanced clinical practitioner in the state of Texas. He was one of the founders of the Texas Chapter of NASW and is a member of CSWE. He also was a member of the National Task Force on Lesbian and Gay Issues of NASW and is a recognized speaker and writer in this field.

**Natalie Jane Woodman** holds an MSS in social work and is an associate professor at the Arizona State University School of Social Work. She is a co-author of *Counseling with Gay Men and Women: A Guide for Facilitating Positive Life-Styles* and is a member of ACSW, co-chair of the Arizona state NASW Committee on Lesbian and Gay Issues, as well as being a member of the Commission on Gay/Lesbian Issues in Social Work Education, CSWE.

**Authors** **Ron Balint** holds an MSW and is a certified social worker licensed by the state of New York.

**Raymond M. Berger,** PhD, is an associate professor in the School of Social Work, University of Illinois at Urbana–Champaign. He has authored numerous articles on aging, as well as the book, *Gay and Gray: The Older Homosexual Man.*

**E. Sue Blume** holds an MSW and is licensed as a certified social worker in the state of New York. She has served as an advisor to the New York State Division of Alcoholism and Alcohol Abuse and is presently in private practice as a psychotherapist, lecturer, and consultant, Long Island, New York.

**Breeze** has had one year of graduate social work education and has worked as a social worker, program developer, and administrator primarily in settings dealing with women's issues and in rural areas. She has been co-chair of the Arizona state NASW Committee on Lesbian and Gay Issues.

**Christian A. Frandsen** holds an MSW, has served as a trainer for a lesbian and gay crisis line in Phoenix, Arizona, and has facilitated lesbian and gay awareness groups at Arizona State University. He has been employed at the Maricopa Medical Center's Psychiatric Crisis Center in Phoenix and currently works in one of the hospital's inpatient psychiatric units. He also has a part-time private practice.

**Bernice Goodman** holds an MS and is a certified social worker licensed by the state of New York and ACSW. She has been a pioneer and prime mover for the rights of lesbians and gays in the social work profession and in the larger society. She has authored books, articles, and monographs on gay and lesbian issues and has gained national recognition as a lecturer, consultant, and expert on the problems of lesbian mothers. She co-chaired the NASW National Task Force on Lesbian and Gay Issues from its inception to its creation as a committee. In the past two years she has been president of the board of directors of the National Lesbian and Gay Health Foundation and co-chair of the National Steering Committee of the Federation of AIDS Related Organizations.

**John Grace** holds an MSW and is the coordinator of the Gay and Lesbian Counseling Program at Family and Children's Service in Minneapolis, Minnesota. He was a member of the advisory committee for this manual.

**Robert O. Hawkins, Jr.,** MEd, Phd candidate, is associate dean and associate professor, School of Allied Health Professions, Health Sciences Center, State University of New York at Stony Brook. He is co-author of *Counseling Lesbian Women and Gay Men*.

**Sue Kaplan** holds a BA in social services and has worked as a counselor for the last five years with lesbians and gay adolescents and runaway youths in San Francisco. She is currently a law student.

**Harry R. Lenna** holds an MSW degree and is presently a doctoral candidate and assistant professor at Arizona State University. He is co-author of *Counseling with Gay Men and Women: A Guide for Facilitating Positive Life-Styles.*

**Kathleen Mayer** is an attorney who for six years has been in private practice in Tucson, Arizona. She has been active in lesbian and gay affairs throughout Arizona and has developed the material in this manual specifically for mental health professionals.

**A. Elfin Moses** holds a doctorate in social work and is an associate professor at the University of Tennessee in Knoxville. She is author of *Identity Management in Lesbian Women* and co-author of *Counseling Lesbian Women and Gay Men.*

**Margaret Nichols** holds a PhD and is a licensed clinical psychologist. She has authored articles on a variety of clinical topics, including gay issues and particularly lesbian sexuality. She is the director of the Institute for Personal Growth, a gay and lesbian counseling center in Highland Park, New Jersey.

**Paul A. Paroski, Jr.,** holds an MD degree and is associate director of the Department of Ambulatory Care, Woodhull Medical and Mental Health Center, Brooklyn, New York. He is founder of Lesbians and Gay People in Medicine, founder and past president of the National Gay Health Education Foundation and board member of the Association of American Physicians for Human Rights.

**Marla A. Petal** holds an MSW degree and was the founder and first director of the Center on Deafness at the Houston, Texas, Center for Independent Living. Practicing in the Los Angeles area, she is a community organizer, advocacy planner, and consultant to consumer organizations.

**Martin Rochlin** holds a PhD in clinical psychology and practices in West Hollywood, California. He is a member of the executive board of the Society for the Psychological Study of Lesbian and Gay Issues, Division 44 of the American Psychological Association.

**Caitlin Conor Ryan**, MSW, is a clinical social worker and organizer. She coordinated the Second National Gay Health Conference, conceived and published the *National Gay Health Directory,* and was the preliminary organizer for the National Gay Health Education Foundation. Currently director of the AIDS Education Fund, Whitman-Walker Clinic, Washington, D.C., she is president-elect of the National Lesbian and Gay Health Foundation and project coordinator of the first national survey of lesbian health care needs. She is also an instructor at Smith College School for Social Work.

**Sue Saperstein**, MFCC, MA, is the founder of Women's Family Services in San Francisco. This clinical and training project is committed to the development of the theory and practice of women's and girls' psychology.

**Fern H. Schwaber** is an attorney in private practice in New York City. She is a member of the board of directors of Lamda Legal Defense and Education Fund, Inc., a not-for-profit gay legal rights organization involved in legal cases across the nation. She was co-coordinator of the 1984 First International Lesbian/Gay Health Conference held in New York City.

**Michael Shernoff** holds an MSW and is executive director of Chelsea Psychotherapy Associates in New York City. He was co-coordinator of the First International Lesbian/Gay Health Conference and authored an article, "Family Therapy for Lesbian and Gay Clients." He is a member of the lesbian and gay advisory committee of the New York City Department of Mental Health, Mental Retardation, and Alcoholism Services.

**Audrey I. Steinhorn** holds a master's degree in social work and is a clinical social work psychotherapist in private practice in New York City. She is chairperson of the Committee on Lesbian and Gay Issues, New York City Chapter, NASW, and is author of several articles on lesbian adolescents and mothers.

**Josephine H. Stewart** is director of psychiatric social work at Methodist Hospital and a private practitioner in Houston, Texas. She has served on the faculty of Indiana University, Ohio State University, University of California at Berkeley, and West Virginia University Graduate School of Social Work. She currently serves as a field instructor for the University of Houston Graduate School of Social Work and as clinical assistant professor, Baylor College of Medicine, Houston. She holds an MSW, ACSW, is a charter member of NASW, is former chair of the Task Force on Lesbian and Gay Issues of the Texas Chapter of NASW, and is chair of the National Committee on Lesbian and Gay Issues of NASW.

**Pat Terry** holds an MSW degree and is an ACSW member. She is manager of the Office of Human Resource Development in the Arizona State Department of Health Services and has been co-chair of the Arizona Chapter's NASW Committee on Lesbian and Gay Issues.

**Gary G. Treese** has an MSW and is a certified social worker–advanced clinical practitioner in private practice in Houston, Texas. He has led a support group for people with AIDS for two years and sees many of these patients and their families in psychotherapy. He has lectured and been a consultant regarding mental health issues for sexual minorities.

**Carol Tully** is an assistant professor of social work at West Virginia University. She has an MSW and a PhD from Virginia Commonwealth University School of Social Work.

**Kirby Wohlander** is former director of counseling at the Community Service Center for the Disabled, Inc., in San Diego, California, and is now in full-time private practice in the San Diego area. He holds an MSW and is licensed by the state of California as a psychotherapist and as a marriage and family counselor. He is a founding member of the San Diego Sex and Disability Task Force.